A True Story About
Life, Music, Love, Loss, and Triumph
from a Traveling Troubadour

That Girl Could Sing

Shannon Price

Dedication

This is dedicated to all those who were on the road and loved it, hated it, or fell under the siren's call of the mesmerizing reverie and made it a lifestyle. To those who tore up hotel rooms and those who tried to make a hotel room home. You know who you are, and this book is dedicated to you, both famous and infamous, to those musicians and friends we met on our travels who we still stay in touch with to say Happy Holidays or Happy Birthday, and to those we call our lifelong friends. I feel confident in saying that none of us would change a thing.

This book is dedicated to my mom, whose goal was for us, her three kids, to pursue all our dreams and passions, which we have done, each to a different extent, even as we age. Thank you to my beautiful, strong mom for never discouraging me from doing exactly what I needed to do in order to become myself. Her unending support still lives on in her spirit, and my steadfast and wise sister who has always supported me in everything I do and still does as she encourages me to keep doing the things I love while she does the same for herself.

This is dedicated to all of you who keep my life full of love and happiness, full of daily excitement, and who inspire me to keep moving forward and to the never-ending new people in my life, especially those who seem like they've always been there. I feel so fortunate to have carried on with this life, meeting and sharing music and life with some famous folks, helping people get some music into their lives, and helping people get healthier and better physically and mentally to live a better quality of life. If I have inspired just one person to be happier and healthier and to find and live their passion, then that is perfect. If that one person has inspired one more person, that's even better. I've loved life, the good and the bad. I used everything that happened as something to learn from.

And to those of us who triumphed and didn't let the long, winding, too-dark, too-bright, hypnotic road taunt us over the years. To those of us who embraced the lifestyle and the addictive freedom and turmoil of the road. After almost twenty years traveling full-time, fifty weeks a year, that road spit me out, a well-respected singer, musician, entertainer, and verified badass who was compelled to leave this lifestyle that I loved and built for one reason: to nurse my longtime, incredibly talented partner, Bruce, through his journey of addiction, bad physical health, mental issues, and eventually, death. It was a true mind-boggle, not knowing what was ahead. Only to find the courage and audacity to start over from scratch, not knowing anything about or having any connection with the other 9-5 life, the daily working man's hours. My head was jumbled, believing that this new life was going to be temporary. At first, I was so internally angry that someone else's self-destructive actions caused this. But I realized that was the choice I had made. This is what I needed to do. But it did not come without strings attached.

I am truly thankful for the life (lives) I've been able to lead and the people who have entered these many lives from the beginning. We learn from everything and everyone. Sometimes, you don't see it until years later, but it comes to you when it's time to remember.

It wasn't luck that I was able to do the things I am passionate about in my life – it was being fearless. Failure was never something that crossed my mind. I just knew I would do these things, and I knew what they were. I didn't always know how to do them, but that never stopped me from figuring it out and doing what it took.

It makes the head, heart, and soul wiser and stronger. Well, it does, and then you realize what it was that you learned from past pain and happiness, and the light finally shines.

The consistent lessons in my life have been love, support, learning, and teaching. My mother let me find my way but never let me do it without her support and wisdom. Even when she was skeptical or fearful of my grand visions, she let me go anyway. She listened to my tales of the road, gave advice when I asked for it, and let me live the life she knew I was supposed to be living. She always said she knew I was coming after my brother was born the year before and the doctors told her it was unadvised to have another child. My sister remembers Mom saying that she needed to have me, and I needed to be born.

Sometimes, life gets in the way of "living," but that's part of it, too. To do what you want to do, you sometimes do what you need to do.

Photo courtesy of Kaylyn Hoskins Photography

Acknowledgment

I extend my heartfelt gratitude to everyone who contributed significantly to the creation of this book. Your support and encouragement have been invaluable throughout this journey.

Special thanks to my late mom, who never stopped letting me explore my passions. To my family, and to my ever-growing family of friends and musicians around the globe who urged and encouraged me to write this book – it's for you. Your unwavering support and understanding during the long hours spent writing and editing and your belief in me fueled my determination. To Mike, who has always made me feel seen and loved. To my friends who sang and played guitars with me throughout junior high and high school, especially Alice and Leanna (R.I.P. my beautiful friend). And above all… to Walter, Roger, Cindy, Ken, Allison, Perry (R.I.P.), Chris and Alex, and all the rest of the boys in the band, for all those decades up to the present. Without you, there would be no stories to tell!

A sincere thank you to Amazon KDP for believing in this project and providing the platform for its publication.

Lastly, to the readers who embark on this literary adventure, your interest in my work is the ultimate reward.

Thank you all for being part of this incredible experience.

Love, Shannon

CONTENTS

About the Author

Shannon Price is an accomplished musician and writer known for compelling storytelling and performing. With a passion for music that began in childhood, Shannon has always been drawn to the power of music and lyrics to transport readers to new worlds and ignite their imaginations.

From the beginning, Shannon Price's musical talent was evident. Constantly relocating, she would find solace on the bench of her family's grand Hammond Organ, effortlessly playing songs she had heard on the radio and television before age five. By twelve, she had mastered the guitar and captivated audiences with her folk songs. At fifteen, she was performing in coffee houses, assembling local bands, and setting her sights on bigger stages.

After college, where she majored in Psychology and Writing at Indiana University, she played with her band full-time, following that lifestyle for almost two decades over the USA and parts of Canada, living in hotels and entertaining in bars, dance halls, and concert settings. Along the way, there was abuse and mistreatment. The bad and the good happened, the delightful and the horrific too, but Shannon became a well-respected singer and a positive force in this world. After writing blogs and getting numerous requests for more, here is her memoir.

In 2016, Shannon's exceptional voice and musical prowess were officially acknowledged when she was inducted into the IA Rock and Roll Hall of Fame for the title of Women Who Rock. This prestigious recognition is a testament to her passion for music and performing, which has garnered her a dedicated following of fans and friends who deeply admire her talent and unwavering dedication.

Shannon's education extends beyond music. She is a fourth-degree Blackbelt in the martial art of Taekwondo, a well-known boxer, and a personal trainer. Her greatest aspiration in this field is to empower women and help them recognize and harness their strength. Shannon is also a successful globally trained hypnotherapist, further demonstrating her commitment to personal development and the empowerment of others.

Page Blank Intentionally

Introduction

My Restless Heart

I was one of the fortunate ones to have been loved unconditionally so I never even considered compromising my ethics and self-respect. You don't need to test yourself or anyone else when you have been raised to be independent and live your passions without doubt or fear. Hopefully, your soul has been learning, all this time, to not hurt others or yourself. I love my family and my family of friends, and I am so thankful that my life has taken me to this place with you all. I chose to be the driver of my life, not a passenger.

If I say I have never been hurt, taken for granted, or abused and misused along the way, that would be very untrue. The struggle is how you learn from those experiences and not let them cling to you or define you. You learn what it is that you want in your life and maybe, more importantly, what you don't want.

It's how you learn to care for yourself and to love and care for others. It's how you strive to be yourself despite the odds; it's how you strive to make others successful leaders when it's time for you to step aside so they can lead the way.

Please don't let time pass you by because that's exactly what will happen. The consequence is that you will have regrets. You'll wonder where that time went. But this is not necessarily a story of life and death. This is a story of change.

And all these years, no matter what was going on personally or professionally, backstage or in a single hotel room, every time I set foot on any stage, it all faded, and only the music and the feeling remained. I remember having the worst arguments and fighting, and every night we stepped up to our instruments, the lights went on, and the drummer counted us in. And in that shimmering, shining moment, nothing else mattered.

I loved airports. Airports used to be so much fun to explore and walking through the shops was exhilarating. They were bustling with excitement, and I always felt safe. Airports are not so comfortable now. Most of all, I truly loved driving to get where we were headed—the landscapes, the sometimes frozen, sometimes melting highways, the exploration. From the deplorable restrooms at the gas station in Pickles Gap, Tennessee to the gigantic truck stops all along the way.

Do you live every day in your small, safe place? Always settling for less of a life than you are so capable of creating and living, maybe because it's just easier and you don't even know what to do or how to begin? What about the experiences you only keep wishing you could have? Maybe you never knew that change was an option.

Jump in! Because, while we are moving forward, we can only look behind to see what we have learned, take what we need and leave the rest of it there. We can never go back, but the memories will stay there for you to revisit. You cannot reinvent the past, and you can't change your memories, but you can reinvent yourself, making new memories, and I hope you do that often. Move forward, always. You have no other choice. Make it worth your while.

Here's to remembering your worth, always.

You are the main character in the book of your life, and whether you're aware of it or not, every page, every chapter, has a piece of wisdom or a lesson to learn to make the next chapter even better and clearer and to make you more open, aware, and tolerant. There will be déjà vu moments to remind you. When that happens, accept it, and try to remember why you needed that reminder. It could be good or not so good. It could be how to do something. It could be about a person, place, or thing, it's something to help you navigate this life.

I wish for you to forever have an awareness of everything that surrounds you – optimism, continued growth, belief in yourself and your abilities, and the strength and determination to achieve anything. See the beauty and light even when others only see the darkness and despair. Trust your instincts. May you live your life with fire and purpose, and may you help others to do the same. Grow every day. Rest and reflect. Educate, Empower, and Evolve. I still believe in love, music, and myself – always.

Photo Credit: Casey K Photos
Lisbon, IA

Chapter 1 – The Beginning Of The Last Day

Running on Empty

December 23, 2001

It had been ten years from the word terminal, an insane, frantic, and utterly unbalanced ten years full of doctors, bad and good, full of being on autopilot. That's how I know for sure that following your passions is always the right way to live.

Because, sometimes, in your life of faithfully pursuing what you always knew was the right pathway of life and staying true to that life, sometimes, when it's time, you will, unequivocally, with or without question, do what you must do in this life by choice or not. Change is inevitable, and I can say I chose my life. I didn't settle for it.

Every year during the holiday season, another lesson of self-renewal presents itself to me. I remember the lessons from all the time before and remember the me I left behind, only to discover there was so much more of me waiting to break out that I never knew existed or counted on.

On December 23rd, 2001, my close friend, Rita, was with me in a hospital room on the sixth floor. We were observing Bruce making his way through the final cycle of life, one of us on each side of the bed railing. It wasn't a sad or grief-stricken feeling; it was not a surprise because, over the years, this was inevitable. It was more like watching in anticipation of what the next step would be in this journey of death after life. And since it was all very peaceful, so were we.

"Could you guys do me a favor?"

Those words came out loud and clear through the gravelly voice where the life support tubes had been inserted for Bruce.

Rita and I looked at each other, "He wasn't talking to us, was he?"

His eyes were closed, but the words were clear.

"Ummm, no, not to us," she said.

Then he uttered this, "I don't want to go just yet. It's not quite time."

It would be at least another fifteen to eighteen hours until it was time.

After so many hours, days, weeks, months, and yes, years in and out of two hospitals, it was a familiar setting. But this time, things were quiet and serene. There was no rushing around by staff, and no one was checking in on us. There were no doctors, no nurses, and no residents or interns looking in or poking and prodding the patient. It was just a very unfamiliar peace, just one single focus. Cousin Judith, a family member who is a master Astrologer, did both Bruce's and my charts and told me that he was waiting for a definite, specific alignment of the planets before leaving. She was spot on. It was uncanny, but the Universe works that way whether you choose to accept that or not.

Next, there was euphoria. Bruce appeared to be speaking to people who were not visible to either of us in that room, but he was answering questions and greeting long-passed people and pets.

Lots of joy was on his face. Then, in one single moment of clarity, he looked over to his left directly at me, and in an ecstatic, rapturous comment, he said, "I really love you."

I heard that loud and clear.

I asked, "Is it time to go?"

He replied, "Almost."

Then, sometime after midnight, December 24th, through the sweat and flush of his face and heavy, immobile, fluid-filled body, I heard,

"I think I have to go now."

"OK," I said.

"I'll be right here."

I waited and watched for any movement or changes. At 5:15 a.m. he exhaled one closing breath, the last song of the night in the last set.

There were no more words. Only the final transition/evolution process remained. It was not sad. There was no anguish or grief portrayed or projected or felt. Only a state of tranquility, placid, sheer peace, and calm remained. My thoughts on this experience are that everyone, at some point, should be in these exact circumstances to see that our own passing is not anything to be afraid to face. It is about the cycle of our lives, remembering that one human's life and his contributions to the human spirit and nothing less and nothing more. This was not a sudden or surprising passing. It was destined, and after those collective tumultuous and tormented years, a peaceful time had finally come.

*"Looking out at the road rushing under my wheels I
don't know how to tell you all just how crazy this life
feels*

Look around for the friends that I used to turn to

*to pull me through. Looking into their eyes, I see
them running, too*

*I'd love to stick around, but I'm running behind
You know I don't even know what I'm hoping to find*

*Running on (running on empty) Running on (running
blind) Running on (running into the sun)*

But I'm running behind" ~ Jackson Browne

5:15 AM December 24th, 2001

Bruce's body took one last exhalation, and then after that was one final movement: the reach of his left arm as if to take someone's hand. This was not random but a purposeful movement. His hands were always beautiful and artistic with perfectly long, musical fingers that could play any instrument he picked up. During the final journey of his physical body, he had not been able to move his limbs for so many days due to thick, heavy fluid throughout his ravaged body. It was simply a voluntary, obvious, and deliberate gesture to reach up and take the hand of another as if being led or guided. Almost simultaneously, this movement was the immediate second after his last climactic breath or even at the same moment. Bruce was left-handed, so it was a natural movement. And there was never any doubt in my mind that his reaching for another hand was truly happening.

That was the end of a short but fierce and profoundly full forty-four years on this planet. Forty-four years that started as a greatly wanted and loved adopted child. Forty-four years of music, genius, energy, brilliance, talent, humor, self-indulgence, self-destruction, gentleness, creativity, then dementia and hallucinations. The final ten of those years were filled with hope, trying to do normal things, like playing instruments and writing music, taking a shower, even talking to others, using his creative instincts, disappointment, searching, hopelessness, experimentation, torture, finding a lost civilization that only he could see and remember, looking for a self that could not be found, and inviting the demons in to stay for good. That led to pain, suffering, the act of forgiving others, forgiving self, euphoria, and finally, peace, something everyone hopes for in the end.

During those years, he was able to accomplish many things. He could play any instrument he picked up with ease, entertaining masses of fans and friends. He wrote and published songs. He learned computer language and programming. He learned the sport of martial arts, wrote me love notes, and left them where I would least expect them. He was an amazing gift-giver. He always paid close attention to each person in his family and to me as well as his friends and always chose perfect gifts. He made lots of artwork resembling a sci-fi movie set. He told me this is where he was before he came to this planet. There were landscapes, animals, and other creatures, and he would draw himself in them too. I still have many of the drawings.

During the last part of those years, there were attempts to stop drinking and recovery weeks in the hospital and other facilities. There were instances of projectile blood vomit, twice leaving a pond of flaming crimson liquid in the hallway between the bedroom and kitchen that made my head spin as I tried to comprehend how to clean it and get 911 on the phone. Once again, the EMTs came in to transfer him to the hospital. I was left to clean up this head-spinning, deep dark red garnet-colored pond the best I could and still be able to breathe. It was as if I were a character in a Stephen King novel.

I only called Bruce's dad once to help me. He was shocked and not sure what to do. He had never seen anything like this. No one understood the severity and hopelessness of this illness, mainly because I didn't share these things. Bruce was adamant about his family not knowing all the terrible things that his body was going through, or at least to the extent of what was happening. And even though I was obliged, I was baffled at how they couldn't see it for themselves when they saw him.

Christmas Eve at 5:15 a.m. brought light snow that was soft, completely silent, and sublime. Rita was there again, and we watched the snow from Bruce's hospital window. When it was time to leave the hospital, I almost forgot that I didn't have to return later since it had been my daily routine for such an uncommonly long, long time. In those hustle and bustle years leading up to this moment, it had become a way of life, just like anything else we do daily, a routine, like a robotic program, constantly reminding myself to breathe.

December 24th, 2001, 6:30 AM

I had the task of making family calls from the phone in the hospital room because now there was only me. It was deemed sort of awkward and uncomfortable, even somewhat disrespectful, for anyone else in his family to be there during the finale. I didn't know why, and I certainly didn't see it the same way. Maybe they didn't want to witness him in this condition.

For a few family members, it was, and always had been, the mindset of 'if I don't see it, it isn't actually happening.' That old silent sentiment: Out of sight, out of mind, and if he's in the hospital, he will get better and get out of there. I can only imagine that what they thought they were seeing in the hospital wasn't the full story.

But what they didn't know, what they never saw, what they will never realize, is that it was never about them and their comfort. It was a final understanding of why, what, how, and a rising enlightenment. It was the end of one man fighting, losing battles, illusions, and me asking myself, how is this even happening? It was never going to end differently. This was a process, and I was the one with the ultimate privilege to witness the event from beginning to end. It was a book of lessons and secrets. The longest chapter of his life happened in those years before 2001. That December was the month of peace, joy, and complete release, which is exactly what December represents. I saw and heard it, but how do you put that into words?

When I got into the car to drive home, I felt a strange wall of calm.

It was as if a light washed over and through me.

I was able to lie down to sleep for a couple of hours before heading to 'make the arrangements' with the family at the funeral home. Janet Jackson's "Shining Down on Me" was on the radio in my car. The Calling, "Wherever You May Go," was on the radio at home. You see, this was all planned as the planets were aligned, just as Judith predicted. Timing is everything.

My home landline phone rang at 10:30 a.m. that same December 24th.

I hesitated to answer. I did, but static was all I could hear. I chuckled because I knew who it was—I still know—and if I had stayed on the line, I would have heard his voice say my name and ask me where he was, where I was, and why he couldn't find me.

Even though he preferred to be cremated, his family wanted him to be buried in their family plot at an epic old cemetery on Church Street in Iowa City where the famous Black Angel monument lives. A simple, beautiful wooden casket made by the Dubuque Monks was chosen because that's what Bruce would have wanted. The steel casing was engraved with a picture of Bruce's Martin guitar. I chose an ethereal smoke marble headstone, all planned in a single morning with his family as if those ten years had an unexpected ending in their eyes. I knew and will forever know things they will never know or see because I was there throughout every second, every struggle.

Bruce spoke to me many times about how he wanted this event to present itself, including the music, what he wanted to wear, and all of the rest.

On the headstone, I asked for these words to be engraved, "Most of us go to our grave with our music still inside of us."

You see, the music doesn't die just because the body of the musician does. His heart seems to beat rhythmically and steadily for eternity.

I know what it feels like to give and get, and that is the only thing I understand. We are all in this together. We breathe the same air. You don't love everyone, of course, but I do know that even if you try to love others, it all comes back to each of us better than before. That's worth it.

A quickly planned memorial service was held on December 27th, 2001, to upwards of 250 musicians, friends, and family from all over the U.S. and beyond. There was an open casket, and people put pictures, CDs, and other special things into the casket. I was saddened to see that they had broken his beautiful fingers to be able to dress him and cross his hands on top of his body. I wasn't prepared for that. It's the only thing I wasn't expecting. I made a CD with songs Bruce had requested months before (because he knew) and songs I wanted him to have. Jackson Browne's 'Running on Empty', which Bruce called his theme song, John Lennon's 'Imagine', Bruce's anthem for diversity and equality, and our favorite classical piece, 'Canon in D' were his most frequently stated requests. Elton John's 'The One' and 'Friends', Angel by Sarah McLachlan because of our life on the road for so many years, living in hotel rooms, and many more lyrics and songs of our life that were so meaningful to us. The service was recorded on a cassette tape as I took a microphone around the room, and everyone had different tales to tell of this brilliant living musician and his life of loving every human, plant, and animal. Funny stories were told, feelings and emotions came out from those you wouldn't expect them from, and it was a real celebration of a life full of music and friendship. When it was over, as we left the service, a group of white birds circled the steeple of the building. Magical. Never miss anything because every single event, everything, means something. Bruce always told me he was going to come back as a bird. You see, he was innately consumed with all things that could fly and took flying lessons at a local airport during the time before his death. And in life, he never missed an opportunity for helicopter and plane rides.

We live, and we learn, or at least we're supposed to. Thanks for everything you taught me, like computer language, electronic repair, how two people could be together 24/7 and have that secret humor, secret silent language, secret anger, unconditional love, and helping me show the world that music is life, and for helping me learn the things I needed to know to carry on with this life including who I was then and who I am now after all this time. Stories never really end. There is a song for every second of our lives, and there's a long story with many chapters and songs that lived before this one that I am about to tell.

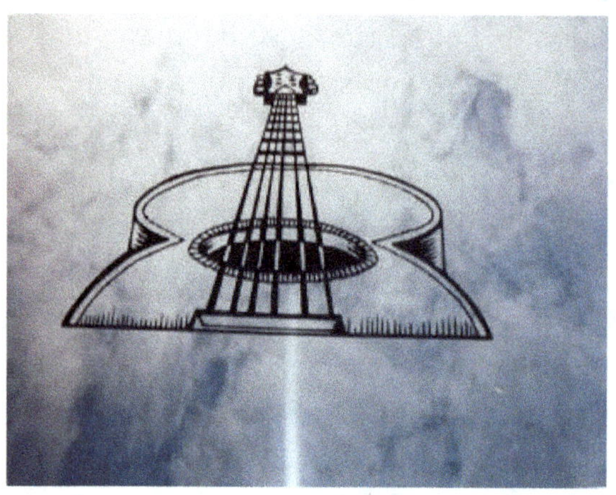

Bruce's metal casket casing with his Martin guitar engraved on the top
(Dec. 27, 2001)

Then The Dreams Began. Vivid Dreams Full of Sound and Color.

That very night of Christmas and beyond, I heard my name called many times in a high-pitched, almost pleading voice in the darkness. These dreams were full of visions. Some were visions of Bruce getting lost. Some visions were of Bruce alive but trying to find the right hotel room or the room where his well-loved bicycle was supposed to be. Others were visions of him being carried off on a gurney and not realizing that he was no longer on this Earthly plane.

He was motionless on the gurney, but his head dropped to one side, and his eyes were fixed on mine looking confused as to where they were taking him, who was taking him, and why. He asked me over and over again,

"Shannon, where am I? Where is my bike?" I heard it loud and clear.

There were so many dreams of us trying to set up the band equipment but not being able to get on or off the right elevators or floors to unload. Not being able to completely set up because a piece of equipment was missing, lost cables, microphones, keyboards, sound system, weather, missing band members. Something was always in the way of completing the setup.

All the rooms in the dream hotels and living conditions had 8s on the doors—88, 888, etc. 8s are numbers of success. I always remember to write down numbers from dreams and then save them. Keeping track of your vivid dreams helps you navigate your waking life.

In dreams, it is said that dogs are protection, and numbers and colors are meaningful. There was one magnificent dream of lush, green countryside with one majestic tree and nothing but tall, green, thick, shiny grass and a fence. Handfuls of seeds were being thrown into the air by an older woman (someone's mother, it felt like), and the seeds turned into birds. There was a dog along the fence in this dream named Mikey. Dogs and other animals were, and still are, in all my dreams. Following far behind me was Bruce having a conversation with another man. The man, who wore glasses, was intently listening. I couldn't see or hear him distinctly, but I seemed to know what they were saying.

In another dream, I was inside a high-rise apartment or hotel, safely looking out of the window to see ice, floods, trucks, and cars being swallowed up by deep apocalyptic flooding waters and holes in the earth. But I was safe from the chaos from my window. And I felt safe, I felt like this wasn't going to cause any distress for me. But I wasn't able to help the others who were caught up in it and signaled to them to come where I was. They couldn't as their vehicles were swallowed up in the flood and open ground.

The giant flying dog from 'The Neverending Story' was the major player in another dream. He was standing over me, protecting me. When his head turned, it was Bruce's face and voice. He told me something important, and I wish I had written it down, but internally, I didn't want to stop the dream.

There were several recurring dreams of villages and towns and people I didn't know, but I knew that I had been there before. The most recurring dream, besides trying to get equipment set up, was one of a warm Southwestern feel and scene. I know it's a place I've been to many times, and it felt like home. The details of color, pottery, and people sitting on steps in these dreams are still in my mind's eye.

I wanted to figure out these dreams because they just kept coming for years. Some dreams were filled with frightening beings and terrifying in remarkably familiar rooms and cabinets with monstrous things and frightening creatures behind the doors. Every dream that included our beloved ferrets was chaotic, the ferrets were running around without a mission. I tried to round them up and get them back in one place, but all they wanted to do was explore and play. There were so many of them (which was actually a real-life situation) and it was arduous and impossible because they were so ambitious.

In another recurring dream, my sister and I were in houses with major water flowing in from the windows and walls. The water was clear, but we couldn't figure out how to stop it. Trying to get down the rickety wooden stairs to the basement was extremely challenging. And there were strange things going on in that basement.

I trusted my instincts and intuition, which are all any of us have in this life to fully trust, even if we don't understand them. Never lose sight of yourself, even if it feels like that is starting to happen and you can't find your way back. See it as a lesson and hopefully see yourself understanding.

It took me about three years to even begin to remember who I was, to find myself again, only a better, more experienced version with much more to follow.

There's always more to the story…both mine and yours.

I lived and loved the gypsy life for almost twenty years, thirteen of those years traveling with Bruce until that terminal illness finally snatched the life of my partner after ten more years of spiraling with what seemed like no way out for him. Twenty-three years is a long time.

That event brought me to Iowa City. This is the place I call home, and it feels that way to me now. I came to live here in the mid-90s and stayed. Holiday Road Band is still here and active locally.

So, let's start at the beginning.

Chapter 2 – From The Beginning

And The Music Begins To Play

I have been invincible and fearless enough to live my life doing the things that I am passionate about, which is more and much different than being enthusiastic about something. But, as I mentioned earlier, I have also done the things I felt that I needed to do when I had to do them. It's not that I was necessarily courageous, but I was curious and full of wonder, and nothing scared me. All I knew were the things I loved. I was unquestionably cut from a different mold, always open to new experiences and exploring everything, everywhere.

My sister, brother, and I were all taught to be this way, but also to be responsible, do well in school, go to college, and always follow our passions wherever they led us.

All my life, the music has been inside of me, outside of me, surrounding me, the biggest part of me since my first day on this planet and probably before that. I know that I was born an old soul. It was always the music that flowed through my veins and energized every cell in this human body. I seemed to know about music and other things like certain animals, books, words, and people before I was old enough to even experience them. Music, making music, and feeling music have always been my biggest passion and it enveloped everything I ever did. I thought everyone was like this.

I spent my days in early grade school living in Colorado. I spent my growing-up years listening to the radio and records, both albums and 45rpms every day whenever I could. My brother and I were given transistor radios one year for Christmas. We would set the dial to a hugely popular station from Oklahoma, KOMA, and no other station came in as clearly and as easily as the great KOMA. At night we went to our rooms and slid the radios under our pillows, listening all night to the most amazing music that became the biggest part of both of us.

It seemed like every song was my favorite. Lightning Strikes by Lou Christie was one of my most loved songs, and I saved my allowance to buy the 45rpm. Of course, the price of a 45rpm at that time wasn't even fifty cents. A full album was around four to five dollars, and if we wanted it, we had to save our own money for it. I loved everything about that record. I loved the beat, the sound of the vocals, and the chord progression, and I listened to it incessantly. Unfortunately, I left that Lou Christie record in the back window of our family car, and it sat in the sun in that rear window and warped like a wave on the ocean. That broke my heart.

I sobbed to my mom, and being the creative mom that she was, she had the perfect solution. She laid it on a soup can or something that size—I don't remember what it was really—and then put it on a baking sheet in the oven. As the sides of my favorite record blossomed like a big black upside-down petunia, she took it out and told me to let it cool.

Like magic, she turned it over, and I had a musical basket to put my bracelets and hair clips in for safekeeping and a perfect display on my dresser. She did not replace the record. The lesson to learn was that it was not a good idea to place a record in the sun and to take care of my belongings. And no one had to tell me that since I saw it in action. I still have that song on a digital download now.

Music is the one thing that was always there, always welcoming, always true blue, and always familiar. As a very young child of four or five years old, I plunked out little tunes by ear on our family keyboard, a big Hammond organ with pedals and drawbars, and sang every song I could remember from the radio.

When I was five years old, my mom asked me if I wanted to take lessons and learn how to play properly. I was five years old, so I said "OK" without totally understanding what "taking lessons" meant. My brother took lessons as well with our beloved teacher, Mr. Kittle. He even held a recital for us on the big screened-in porch of his home. The Hammond was on the left side, and the piano on the right.

We had all the best Broadway albums: West Side Story, The Unsinkable Molly Brown, Camelot, South Pacific, The Sound of Music, Gypsy, My Fair Lady, The Music Man, Oklahoma, and a million more. I knew all the songs and all the lyrics and couldn't get enough. Then came Elvis movie soundtracks. I loved all of it, even to this day. However, at age nine, in February 1964, everything changed.

I was nine, and my brother was ten. The Beatles were on the Ed Sullivan Show and my brother and I were glued to the television, mesmerized by the sound and look of the Fab Four. What were we watching? What were we listening to? We sat on the floor right in front of the television and moved up closer and closer until we felt like we were swallowed up into the front row of the Ed Sullivan audience.

I don't even remember our mom telling us to back up a little. We were hooked for life. Our creative instincts kicked in, as they did for a million other kids in 1964. We imitated our own imaginary band to Beatles records, wearing our bathrobes backward so we could have

Nehru collars like the Fab Four. I think you see where this is going and how it changed the way I spent my entire life. I was never one of those screaming teenage girls. I was more interested in the full harmonies and vocals and the way they played their instruments. I noticed how Paul played his bass. It was on the other side - left-handed. I was drawn in watching how they engaged people with their stage presence. I loved all four Beatles for many reasons and knew instinctively that this was new and life-altering. I wanted to be just like them. Throughout my life, I was fascinated and absorbed with all vocals, how instruments were played, and the stage presence of each member of any group.

My plum-painted bedroom, which had exquisite, delicate Edgar Degas ballet posters that I loved, turned into a preteen Beatles shrine. Suddenly, there were Beatles posters where the graceful, rhythmic Degas dance posters once hung. There were Beatles bobbleheads and albums in my room.

The only other things in that room were my massive amounts of Barbies and her family, a small suitcase stuffed with handmade clothes just for Barbie, which was a gift from my mom on one of my birthdays. Barbie loved dressing up for her dates, but not with the multitudes of Ken dolls that awaited her presence, but for movie stars and rock stars.

When I was about eleven, I wanted to be a folk singer. If I loved something, I would become truly passionate and obsessed with it. I put on my records, listened to the radio constantly, and sang harmony with all my favorite artists. I found that the notes came easily and naturally, and harmonizing felt exciting, like nothing I ever knew.

Singing and harmonizing are fulfilling, hypnotic, and engrossing. I loved all the music, melodies, and words to each song. My love of folk music has never left me. Sitting in my bedroom for hours on end, I would sing and eventually learn to play the guitar so I could play all the songs by Peter, Paul and Mary, Bob Dylan, the New Christie Minstrels, Joan Baez, Simon and Garfunkel, Donovan, The Byrds, Joni Mitchell, James Taylor, Linda Ronstadt, and of course my favorite harmonies were Beatles songs. I loved them all. I even imagined a big half-circle of chairs as I would perform for my imaginary audience.

Who am I?

"Yesterday, a child came out to wander, Caught a dragonfly inside a star

Fearful when the sky was full of thunder And tearful at the falling of a star

And the seasons, they go round and round

And the painted ponies go up and down

We're captive on the carousel of time

We can't return; we can only look Behind, from where we came,

And go round and round and round in the circle game."

~Joni Mitchell

Welcome to my life. I'm Shannon, also known as Shanno, Shan, Shanny, Kitty, Kat, Ms. Price, and Kit. I never doubted who I was, or where I was going in this life. I was always completely focused on what I wanted in my life but was sometimes unaware of what surrounded me because of my direction of focus.

Shannon Price First Grade 1960

We moved several times while I was growing up. My father was in newspaper advertising and changed jobs frequently, not giving any thought to the fact that the whole family had to be uprooted and do the same. I was told later that it was because he was always in debt and trying to outrun his debtors. I believe that is due to the times of the 1950s and 1960s when he kept moving our family from state to state, changing addresses, and there was no way to contact him. But moving, meeting new people, and making new friends was probably part of my need to entertain people so they would accept me, so I would fit in, and have a sense of belonging.

We weren't a religious family, but my father, who was raised in the Jewish faith, loved to take us all to church on Easter, and that was the only time my brother and I ever went as children and teenagers. I don't ever remember going to Synagogue on any occasion. During the holiday season, we decorated with both Christmas and Hannukah symbols, and I loved my father's menorah and the spinning angels on a smaller candelabra. My brother and I never thought anything about it. We were preoccupied with sharing the newest Big Fat Sears catalog and making our Christmas lists.

I was born incredibly nearsighted and could not see except for blurry blobs. I was bullied in childhood because of my outrageously thick and always getting thicker glasses. I remember being at a movie theater with my family when I was just a toddler. I crawled under the seat and fell asleep since I couldn't see the movie. My mom picked me up and kept me in her lap.

In the third grade, I wore bifocals, and by the fifth grade, I was wearing trifocals. Of course, there were no compressed lenses, so everyone could see the lines on those lenses as my glasses got thicker and heavier until the eye doctor asked my mom what she thought of putting me in contact lenses at age twelve or thirteen since my vision was getting progressively worse.

She said yes to that eye doctor and told me I had to do the process exactly as he instructed. After the first couple of weeks of wearing the hard contacts, they began to fall out of my eyes for what appeared to be no reason. Heading back to the eye doctor, he told us that my eye shape was changing and improving quickly with contact lenses. My flat eyes were finally becoming rounder instead of flat in shape and were more stable. So, he adjusted the prescription, and I never looked back. Even though I had to wear glasses whenever I took out the contact lenses, I didn't have to wear them during school or any other time except for swimming.

Because there are mean people of all ages and at all stages of our lives, I find it sadly interesting but tragic that when people see someone with very thick glasses or any other obstacle, they assume they are also below standards in intellect and perceive them to lack certain skills and savoir-faire, even when that perception is so wrong.

Lack of vision may have been the reason my depth perception has been a little off during my life. Ever since I can remember, I have been running into walls and doors, hitting my head while getting in and out of cars, and smacking my elbows, hands, and knees for no reason just by walking or turning in a chair.

My mom always said... "well, there she goes."

Thank goodness, nothing serious ever came from it, but still, I have no idea why this happens. When Bruce and I were just starting out, he would say, "OH, are you OK??"

Of course, I was OK with a bump on my head or a roll of my ankle. Not too long after, he would just chuckle and say, "She did it again."

As a child, I would just take off down the hall and run into a wall or a doorknob by turning too fast or missing my turn by just that much. I still do that. But the worst one of my childhood dumb accidents I recall was the day my brother and I went to the park across the street after school to wait for our mom to pick us up. There was one of those kid-powered merry-go-rounds where some kids got on, and the other kids ran to spin it around and then jump on. I was one of the kids riding on the merry-go-round. I saw my mom walking up to get us, and of course, I let go of the railing to wave to my mom. I went flying face first from that ride into the gravel below. I think my glasses flew across the park. I will never forget the sound she made at that moment. It was a gasp that was very loud and almost silent at the same time.

I've only heard that sound of terror from her a few times as I grew up. I got up like nothing happened as warm blood was dripping down my face. It wasn't anything serious, only a couple of scrapes from the gravel, but my mom's face is one thing I will never forget. I didn't even know I was bleeding because I was so happy and smiling to see my mom. Did I ever ride the kid-powered merry-go-round again? Of course, but my brother was supposed to keep an eye on me at all times.

My very favorite television show was the early Saturday morning show Where the Action Is. All the stars of the show had me starstruck. Dick Clark was the host (this was a spinoff show of American Bandstand, my other favorite show, of course). There was Steve Alaimo, Paul Revere and the Raiders, the Action Kids dancers, and every music star you could name, and then some. My parents took me to a live Where the Action Is concert for my twelfth birthday. It was my very first real concert. I got to experience Paul Revere and the Raiders, Steve Alaimo was hosting, the dancers were there, and the concert I went to also had Little Stevie Wonder in the lineup. I was hanging over the balcony seat and didn't sit back even once during the show. I never missed an episode on Saturday mornings, and now I was right there. I wanted to be a performer on the show.

One Saturday morning in about 1965, when, the paperboy (remember the paperboy collections) came to the door. He rang the doorbell, and I did not want him to see me in my pj's sitting on the floor, watching Where the Action Is. I ran up the stairs, and halfway up, I slammed my big toe into the next step and had to dip down and hide while my mom was at the door with the paperboy. Yes, I broke that toe. And I can't count the times I have rolled my ankles throughout my life. I often wondered why I was the only person to step in that one hole on the softball field. It even happened when I was just walking onto an elevator. (I figured out it was my platform shoes, but my foot specialist says it's from my high arches). It happened countless times in my life. These days, I always seem to be bumping into doors, or I have a smashed or pinched finger from putting weights on a bar or lifting dumbbells off the rack and putting them back on the rack. So, if you see me run into a wall or pinch my fingers with weights, no worries, and if you see me bump my head, no worries. But if I go flying off into the gravel, please help me up.

No one in my family was born in the same state. I am the youngest of three kids in my immediate family and was born in Dodge City, Kansas. My mom was born in Cheyenne, Wyoming. She was a beauty her entire life with her chestnut brown hair and crystal blue eyes. She was thin, with long arms and legs, and I loved her beautiful hands. Her fingers were long, willowy, and graceful, and when she reached her 60s, her index finger on her right hand developed a bend at the first joint. My sister and I both inherited that, but we feel it bonds all of us. My mom always seemed very tall in my eyes, that is, until I got older. Then we were the same height, which was only five-foot-five, and now I am a little shorter by an inch or so. When my twenty-ninth birthday rolled around, I loved hearing her say about all three of us – me, my sister, and herself, "Isn't it nice we're all the same age now?" She was not someone who dressed lavishly or upscale elegantly but always looked put together and had a graceful, elegant stride. Her favorite color was blue, and she used a lot of blues, greens, and earthy browns in her paintings.

One of Mom's painted tiles.

She taught me how to dress, wear makeup, and everything young girls want to know about such things. She let me experiment with hairstyles, but I loved my hip-length hair in braids the most. When she was young, modeling was her career, although she had always wanted to go to law school, but, as it does, life got in her way and even though she attended college, she was never able to go to law school. She met my father in California when she was modeling, and he was in newspaper advertising. She was smart, creative, an artist of all things, and most of all, a wonderful teacher. Her three children always came first, no matter what, making her a natural mother, and she was proud of that title.

There was always a mysterious air about my mom. I never knew any of my relatives, which I feel was deliberate by design, but I never worried or questioned why while growing up. All my friends spoke of getting together with cousins, aunts, and uncles, but it sort of blew past me without a second thought.

My father, who was born and raised in the Bronx, New York, was olive-skinned with dark, shiny, glass-like black eyes and very long eyelashes, black hair, and he was extremely attractive. Growing up, he seemed to dote on bringing us gifts after coming home from a business trip or wherever he had been. He always, without fail, brought me record albums when I was in grade school. These were great albums from artists such as the Kinks, Dave Clark Five, Paul Revere and the Raiders, and more. He must have paid attention to my musical obsession and sensed who I was going to be.

On one trip, he brought me go-go boots. They were perfect, white, and just like the ones Nancy Sinatra wore, as did the girls on Hullabaloo, Where the Action Is, and Goldie Hawn on Laugh-In. He smoked a pipe and cigars and every weekend, let my brother and me choose whatever tobacco we thought smelled good from the pipe store. Then, we got to choose a comic book and a treat. My brother chose Superhero comics or Mad Magazine, and I always chose Archie comics and any comics related to Archie and the gang.

I don't remember ever feeling completely comfortable around our father, but I didn't realize what I was feeling were my instincts kicking in. My brother felt the same way. We had a fine life as kids, lots of Christmas presents and birthday parties, and we played a variety of sports. I even had one of the first Barbie Dream Houses. As a kid, I never thought about money, but I assume this was one of the reasons he was in so much debt. I wish I had known more about the relationship between my parents. Nevertheless, I was born last and always lived happily in my private little world.

My blonde, green-eyed older sister, who is ten years my senior, had a different birth father and was born in Fullerton, California. She lived an outdoor western, horseback riding, native type of life growing up as I had envisioned from all the photos I had seen over the years. My sister was never around a lot since she was older and in school, college, and the Navy.

In my eyes, she was mysterious, smart, and beautiful. I wanted to do everything she did, even cutting my Crystal Gayle-length hair when I was eight or nine because I wanted a Pixie Cut just like she had. If I remember correctly, the hairstylist saved my long hair, which she had put into a ponytail to cut. My mom held back her tears but let me find out for myself if I liked it. Yes, I did like it until school picture time. I didn't like the picture of me with that short hair. When it started to grow back, I just let it grow. I seldom cut it after that except for trims until I was at least in my early thirties.

My brother, who is one year older, was born in Las Vegas (Nevada of course, even though Las Vegas seems like its own state). My brother and I hung out together all through our childhood and teen years. We looked so much alike that people thought we were twins. Usually, you never saw one of us without the other during our youth. We had pets together, picked on each other, we both played music, walked and rode our bikes to school and in the summer, to the pool. He would tell me which boys were OK to go out with and which boys were not, but we were always there for each other. When he left for college, it was strange at first, but I relished the fact that I was having one-on-one time with my mom.

My family moved frequently from the time I was very young until I was in junior high school. The only place I have a clear memory of as a crawling baby is from when we lived in Alamogordo, New Mexico.

I remember this because as a saggy diaper, crawling, just learning to walk toddler, and curious about everything, I was about to grab a scorpion until a piercing shriek came from my mom (as all moms do when their child is in danger or even perceived danger). She made one gasp and then a booming "NO," which is all I remember. It was at that moment I was completely repulsed and repelled by just about any type of bug. And it sticks with me even today, especially when it comes to dreaded grasshoppers. That might sound insignificant, but there was an incident later when I was sixteen.

Sitting in a lawn chair one summer day, on the hill behind our house, overlooking a small natural pond, I was suddenly and without warning, surrounded by jumping and flying grasshoppers. It felt like an Alfred Hitchcock movie and I was the star of the scene. I can still see it happening and it feels like I was watching myself jumping up, swatting, and screaming. I was shaking when I got back to the house. Who knew Indiana grasshoppers were so big and could fly so high?

We moved to a few different states growing up and spent the longest amount of time in Grand Junction, Colorado, until Junior High, when we finally moved to Indiana. I still remember my address in Grand Junction and how we loved to ride our bikes up and down the street for what seemed like hours with the neighborhood kids, go to the roller-skating rink several days a week in the Summer, where my brother and I, along with a couple of other teens and pre-teens went every single Saturday morning and got to help adults and children learn how to skate. We had a blast, and my favorite part was the break time when everyone would get soda and peanuts. I always got Dr. Pepper or cream soda and we all put peanuts into the bottles of soda and watched the salt from the peanuts make it fizz. That was such a treat.

I loved to sneak into my older sister's room and admire her record albums, which fed into and encouraged my love of folk music and early rock and soul, wishing I could wear her cool, swirling high school skirts and clothes, play her records, and sing and dance. I always tried my best to put everything back exactly where it was, but I knew she was on to me. She had only the best music, like Johnny Mathis, Peter, Paul, and Mary, and so many more. I hope she still has them in her LP collection, which is vast and has amazing vinyl records, including Broadway, classical, jazz, folk, and any music you could ever imagine.

I will never forget the time my sister, who was home from college for the weekend, when she and one of her friends took me with them to a department store. They were ten years older, and I felt so grown up hanging out with those college girls. I had a blast, especially when my sister noticed the store had a record album playing on one of those old consoles just like we had in our house, with the record player, television, and radio all in one piece of furniture. She decided that the music must have been pretty boring because she grabbed a record from the shelf. It was Junior Walker and the All-Stars. She put it on the console and played the tune Shotgun.

The next thing I remember is that I was nervous, looking around, and wondered if we should just leave, but then I realized we were all dancing right there in the store.

By then we figured we had better get out of there before someone found out it was us who had changed the music. It's still one of my most cherished and fun memories. And I still love the song. My sister always had the best taste in music.

When I was in the fifth grade, a girl in my class asked me if I wanted to downtown to get pompoms and cheer for our football and basketball teams at our elementary school. Of course, I said Yes, because it would be entertaining and fun, and I was just happy that she asked me to do something with her.

We planned to have her mom take us downtown to the store we wanted to go to and then bring me right home. My parents were at work during the day, and since I figured I would be home before they were going to be, I went. If I remember correctly, no one was home. Our parents were at work, and my brother was at swimming or football practice. I was very independent and saw no harm anyway, so off we went to get our pom poms.

After we bought the glistening cheer-makers, I said thank you to her mom and said I needed to get home. It seemed like it was already getting a little dark, so I was in a hurry to get home and not get into trouble. It just figures that her mom said she needed to stop at the bank before taking me home. Then she had to make another stop for something. Boy was I going to be in trouble!

It was about six o'clock or later when I finally got home. I jumped out of the car and ran up to the front door, which was unlocked. Now, that was strange, because we always locked the front door. I had no key with me, so I was glad it was open. To my surprise, no one at all was there. I was calling to each room for everyone, but there was no answer, only an empty house. Remember, there were no cell phones and no computers in the 1960s, and there wasn't a payphone in sight on the car ride to let them know I would be home soon.

I just sat and waited. In a short time, everyone rushed into the house, and my mom reached out, grabbed me, and held me tight. They had no idea where I was or what happened, and of course, I was grounded. My independent streak shone out loud that day. I don't remember my friend's name, but I can still envision her mom's face looking at us in the back seat and riding in her car.

I was forever curious and needed to explore everything, anywhere, anytime. I wanted to know the answers to all the questions of the universe. My brother and I spent many hours at a big vacant lot close to our house. Sometimes, I would just wander off there alone to see what archeological finds I could dig up. There were always arrowheads, cool rocks, soda bottle tops, coins, wires, screws, nails, and big treasures that would make my mind wander. Where did these come from? Who had them last? How ancient were these things? Did they fall from space? My brother and I would put them in our pockets, save them, and take them home. I know our mom tossed out the junk and kept the arrowheads and rocks for us because we didn't miss the other stuff. Those were the actual real treasures after all.

I have always been very independent, adventurous, and free-spirited, and I was very sociable in school, even though I usually felt like I was in my private little world and didn't quite fit in with other groups of kids. I seriously wanted to fit in, so I became the entertainer, always hoping to make everyone happy. Even at a young age, I knew I had other things to do with my life. So many times, I tried my best to encourage everyone to like me and do the things I liked and did, thinking it would make them happy, too. Maybe the best way to do that was through music. Nothing was more important than the music.

I have always loved folk music, and I wanted to be a folk singer. I would sit in my room for hours on end singing and playing the guitar that my father had but never used, learning all the songs by the New Christie Minstrels, Joan Baez, Woody Guthrie, Pete Seeger, Joni Mitchell, and all the greats, and spent all my time playing instruments and singing everything from folk music to pop and rock, recruiting my friends and their friends to sing with me and play guitars, forming bands and playing in garages for friends and playing for parties and weddings throughout my teen years and college. From bars to concert halls, large and small venues, to this day, I've always been much more comfortable on a stage in front of a crowd rather than individually in a group or party situation. We are, in this family, born entertainers.

It seemed so natural to me that I simply wanted my friends to feel that same elation and joy I felt. We were all listening to the same records and the same songs on the radio. It was always the one place I knew I belonged. It was the one place I didn't have to compete to be the best or to be part of a group. I could just be me.

I had already taken lessons on the Hammond Organ, not the piano like most kids. I liked the sound of the organ, the double keyboards, the drawbars, and the pedals. In the seventh grade, at school, I took lessons on the violin, mainly because I wanted to do everything my big sister did, and she played the violin. I wanted to be in the school orchestra, not the school band. Brass instruments did not interest me, even though I loved every bit of the Motown sound and brass bands like Chicago as they appeared on my radar throughout the years.

It was in the seventh grade that we moved to southern Indiana. That was the place my brother and I called our home all through Junior High, High School, and College. Once we got to Indiana, my superhuman, extraordinarily wise mom put her foot down with my father. She declared that now we were in Junior high, we were not moving again. She wanted us to have real friends and develop those relationships. And that is exactly what we did.

My father had other so-called ambitions. He was seldom around, which seemed to be just fine with all of us except my mom. I could feel her anger, sadness, and stress towards him like it was part of me. When I was about thirteen, they parted ways for good and divorced. In 1972, when it was time for my high school graduation, I received a phone call from him. It was the first time I had heard from him in at least three or four years. All he wanted to know was if I was going to college. I had two scholarships, so yes, I was going. I found out later that he was checking to find out if he still needed to pay child support, which was a bit sketchy because he rarely paid the amount that was required anyway, if at all. I suppose he didn't want to get into legal trouble.

Our father was a newspaper advertising guru but had some dealings on the side that we weren't aware of. It seems that he was always trying to outrun his debts and who knows what else. This is one reason we were always moving, as I learned later in life. He also had more than one family and several children none of us knew about. When we were in grade school, he took our college savings account money, and he also took my mom's wedding ring, which had little diamond stars and rubies embedded in it. He removed and sold some of the tiny rubies and diamonds. My mom gave me her ring before she passed. I always thought it was just beautiful. Some of the stones are missing, but it is full of my mom's spirit.

During our early time in Indiana, when my brother and I were in seventh and eighth grades, we decided that we wanted to have a little "party" for our new friends in the neighborhood since we were, literally, the new kids on the block. Without hesitating, my mom said that we could, with this stipulation: once we were able to be the entertainment for our party it could happen. We were musical and always had been, and we were also very theatrical and dramatic. Of course, most kids are at that age, but we milked it since we were encouraged to entertain by making up short skits to perform in front of our parents and their friends. So, we got out our records and made a little plan.

In the house, was that beautiful Hammond organ and a guitar that was our father's. I don't ever remember seeing or hearing him play it. We were also in charge of refreshments. I'm not sure if I remember it all correctly, but I knew my brother was going to put a little band together with his friends, The Boys, as I called them. They came over to begin practicing, and I could not figure out why they didn't want me to join them. This was supposed to be our party, so it was only reasonable to me that I would be in the band too. They did not invite me to be in their band because I was a girl and his little sister. I remember very little about that little band except they had one or two practices at our house. I don't think that little neighborhood party ever happened, but The Boys sure had fun. I watched them and wanted to do that so much.

After that, I picked up the guitar that my father never touched, plinked around on it, and taught myself from what I heard on my records. My mom got me a tried-and-true Mel Bay book of guitar chords to learn how to play correctly since we couldn't afford lessons. I would just shut my bedroom door and play for hours, learning where to put my fingers on the strings to make chords until I remembered them, and my fingers automatically went to the right places.

I accomplished several chords and learned some songs. I didn't even notice how my fingers hurt from all the hours of working on those songs. I could see how red and tender they were, and then the skin on my fingers started to peel. It was all part of the process. The very first song I learned was "Today, While the Blossoms Still Cling to the Vine." There were only a few chords, so it was easy to learn and memorize. Then, it was on to Joan Baez, Peter, Paul and Mary, Joni Mitchell, Linda Ronstadt, James Taylor, John Denver, Carly Simon, Bob Dylan, Neil Young, and whatever else I could sing and play.

My most cherished instrument was a 12-string guitar, a birthday gift from my sister. I could not believe my eyes and ears. It went with me everywhere. It took longer for me to tune it and change strings, and it was worth every second. I have no idea what happened to my father's old guitar.

We had a cool little music store in New Albany, Indiana, where my brother had a part-time job after school and in the summer for about a year. He brought home a banjo one day that he purchased. I couldn't stop myself from picking it up and learning how to play it, and that's exactly what I did. I learned from a book and taught myself two songs. I didn't stick with it because I wanted to play my guitar. But I will never forget how much fun it was, how it sounded, and how generous it was for my brother, who was a woodwind player, to share it with me.

The high school choir was wonderful. Our teacher, Mr. Neely, was loved by everyone and was an outstanding director. As we sat in our assigned seats, according to our vocal range, we knew to listen to him and learn the parts for our sections. When it came time to put it all together, he was brilliant. It was everyone's favorite class.

During choir practice, he had us do what he called "Choir Calisthenics," in which we would turn in one direction and pound our fists on each other's upper back, then turn and do the same to the other person. It was fun, made us laugh, and opened our singing apparatuses so the sound became much bigger and surprised everyone in the class.

We had one of the first "swing choirs" in the area. Each person who wanted in had to audition. I got in since I was able to sing from tenor to soprano, but I was placed in the alto section regularly. We sang all types of music, but for this group, Mr. Neely especially loved the pop music of our era, including I'd Like to Teach the World to Sing, and songs like Cherish by The Association, and other songs from the late 1960s and early 70s. Besides school concerts, we got to travel to other schools and businesses to perform on some days which, in turn, let us out of school for the morning on those days.

For our senior year, we performed music from Jesus Christ Superstar, and I got the solo, "I Don't Know How to Love Him," which I practiced hard to be able to perform well. He also set it up so our choir could record an album of classical, pop, and show music.

It was recorded in a beautiful church with amazing acoustics. A boy named Danny and I got to record the song "If" by Bread on that album. Danny played the guitar, and I sang the song. It was an extraordinary time of my life and right in line with everything I wanted to do.

During this time, our mom had been raising us on her own. I was the youngest and maybe the most free-spirited and independent of all of us, next to my sister, who most certainly went her own way during her life. My other friends from school who were not in the cliques, or the in-crowds were the ones I liked to hang out with the most. They had no discouraging attitudes, and they were so genuine. It was always much more natural to just hang out and be with those kids who didn't seem to have a "group," and had nothing to prove.

Not everyone will be in your tribe, but you should always trust your instincts. They were genuine friends and still are today. I had a few best friends that I spent all my time with, like Alice and Leanna (who unfortunately passed away during the writing of this book), who would sing with me, walk back and forth to our houses, talk about music and boys, and hang out at the pool with our baby oil, Sea and Ski, along with baby's butt Desitin zinc for our sunburned noses. We all got on just fine and helped each other grow into what we were going to become. I'm so grateful that we can keep in touch on social media.

As we grew up and were getting close to graduation age, some of my closest friends were going to college, and some were getting married and having kids right away, but no one else had decided to make a life of music and the spellbinding call of the road except for me. A few of my friends were killed in the Vietnam War, some perished in auto accidents, and one kid 'hopped a train,' as we called it, and went wherever it took him one summer. Other friends were getting engaged, married, or pregnant. Time seemed to keep moving, and my life plan never changed.

Mom had a job that I believe she truly liked as a director at a special education school. When my mom was younger, she wanted to become a lawyer or a teacher. That didn't work out due to some family circumstances. But she was a natural mother and teacher, and she was an incredible artist, a painter of beauty in the outdoors, landscapes, flowers, animals on canvas, tiles, and anything else she wanted to experiment with, like my t-shirts and sweatshirts that I asked her to paint on.

Throughout my life, my mom never wanted to let me know if she was sick or hurt. When I was living away from home, my mom moved to Houston with my sister, which I knew was the best thing for her. When I would call, and mom couldn't talk because she was busy or she did speak to me but sounded just a little bit off, I had to probe my sister to tell me what was going on. The answer was usually that mom fell from a ladder, or that she had the flu, or had an accident of some kind. It took me a long time to decode and interpret this odd action. Before I was born and my mom was raising my older sister alone, her mother had a life-altering accident. Her mother, one of the late grandmothers that I never knew, (as I mentioned previously, I didn't know any of my grandparents or uncles, aunts, or cousins, for various reasons), had to live with my mom, so she and my sister, who was young at that time, could help take care of her. I truly believe she thought it was a burden, and she never wanted that for us. There are a lot of family tales that I never knew until much later in life, and some I still don't know. My mom passed away in 2008 from a heart condition no one knew she had. She was eighty-five. Sometimes, I can see her dancing and laughing with Bruce. They were very good friends, and I expect that they are always around me.

My brother, who is a year older, was a theatre and speech major in college. He acted and sang in many productions, eventually teaching theatre and directing plays. He went on to direct a production at Disneyworld and Universal Studios in Orlando. He's now retired but still volunteers and fills in at Universal Park and loves it. He is one hundred percent Disney, always has been, and is good at it. He is a phenomenal dad and husband, which is the direct opposite of what we saw in our father. I have always been my brother's biggest fan, well, besides his fabulous wife, who is the love of his life. Considering he was raised by a mom and two sisters, then got married, and has two daughters, a granddaughter, and one grandson. He knows how to treat women and how to raise them, and both of my nieces have wonderful husbands.

I majored in psychology and writing in college. Even with other things swimming around in my head, like forensics and criminal justice, and getting good, almost perfect grades, my music took first billing. It's as if none of the other things mattered and I was only along for the ride but needed to get on with it.

My sister lived away most of my life. She always had her own life, which I thought was very exciting. I loved her visits, and I loved it when I got to visit her in places she lived, like New Orleans and her long-term home, Houston, which is my second home as well. We had family turmoil like any other family, but it seemed to us that being together was more important. We supported each other in any endeavor we could pursue, and she helped raise me and took good care of me so many times. She still does. I never knew anything much about my sister's life. That ten-year age difference meant that she didn't have much in common with a kid my age. Even though she was always away at college, living in another state, or in the Navy, my sister always seemed to be able to take care of me no matter what. When our mom passed away in 2008, we sat in her house on the sofa with her big, beautiful black Rottweiler, Hannah, and went through everything in our mom's rectangular metal lock box. Our mom always called it the strong box, and as a child, I loved that mysterious box.

In my eyes, the most significant piece of my mom's history in that box was a photo of her. It was a black and white headshot when she was younger and modeling. I'd never seen anything so beautiful, and as a child, I opened the box a million times just to see that photo. For some reason after modeling, she disliked having her picture taken for any reason. I never questioned it.

I knew there was more to the box, and I didn't think anything else would ever be so important to me as that photo. But after our mom's passing, when my sister and I sat to open the box together, there were so many pieces of our lives in that box. Every single report card from all of us kids was in that box. Our grades were always at the top of the class, but I was dinged more than once for talking in class during grade school if you can imagine.

Also inside that box we found our maternal grandparents' wedding invitation with their photo and dried flowers inside. I had never known my mom's parents, so this struck me as something incredibly special. There were envelopes with baby hair and teeth from all three of us. These things were all very well preserved and precious to us as we removed each artifact carefully to observe.

There were also photos of all three of us, from babies to college graduates. My sister had been looking for some photos that she was positive our mom had kept because she was making photo albums of each of us. Those pictures were not there, but she knew they had to be somewhere in the house. Mom was very protective of us and never wanted the wrong people to find us or know where we were. I don't know the complete story of any of this or who those wrong people might be, but it had to do with my father and debt and her father with something about crime mobs and a suspicious car crash where he was killed. I'm not even sure how we can research that these days. My sister finally found those old photos taped to the underside of a chair when she had to stand on that chair to reach the top shelf for a book she needed. All we could do was laugh and say, "Of course."

Meeting Marcus

Music and entertaining anyone who would listen or watch us always came naturally to all three of us kids. I started to sing and play keyboards at the age of five, then guitar at the age of ten, and put local bands together starting at the ripe old age of fifteen. This leads to my stories of Marcus, (not his real name).

Marcus and I went to the same high school. When we met in 1968, I was a freshman, and he was a senior. He was the captain of the high school basketball team, and yes, I already knew who he was, everyone did. That's the only thing I knew about him at the time: the basketball captain. He was very tall, with dark, naturally wavy hair, but he preferred to blow dry and brush straighten it. He had green eyes, as I do, and that dazzling white Pepsodent smile. Remember Pepsodent toothpaste commercials? He walked up to me in the hallway, towering over me, looked me in the eyes, and told me that I was the girl he was going to marry.

My reaction was a thought of, "What did he just say?" which then turned into a silly, giggly, blushing situation. I was with one of my friends, Kathy, walking to our class, and she heard everything. It was something we gossiped about together for the rest of that school year. As Marcus and I talked in frequent walks down the school hallways, (he always seemed to know where to find me). I discovered that he was a guitar player, about three years older, and would be graduating that coming spring in 1969.

Time passed as it always does in high school. I was busy with everything from choir to class assignments, learning my instruments and the lyrics to all my favorite songs, baton twirling, and swimming practices, playing records, and all those things that teenagers did before there were social media. We interacted with each other in person and on the only phones we had, which were landlines and party lines, so we talked and whispered about school, life, boys, and everything else on those phones and hoped nobody in the house could hear us. The phone cords were usually long and squiggly so we could pull the reciever into our rooms and shut the door. Some of my friends had personal phones in their bedrooms. That was dreamy.

Twirling Baton in high school circa 1971

Like most high school girls, I loved writing poetry and turning it into song lyrics. In the tenth or eleventh grade, a teacher ran an after-school guitar club that I joined. Our assignment was to take a certain chord progression and see if we could write a song. Only three of us did. Sadly, the teacher made fun of the songs we had written instead of actually knowing how to guide us and help us, and then just blew it off. He probably wasn't thinking that his statement might impact us for life. I genuinely don't believe he meant it to be derogatory, but I certainly took the comment as such. And I am also sure he didn't know how to write lyrics and help us put a real song together. That action was the biggest factor in my decision to keep all my lyric writing to myself and not let anyone see it or hear it. Which is exactly what I did with any of the songs I wrote after that. Then I just didn't write songs so much at all anymore. He never knew how his words affected my confidence, and not in a good way. However, I did keep a notebook of lyric pieces that I kept, and later on, while traveling with Bruce, we wrote several songs together, many with funny lyrics that we made into songs just for us. It was a wonderful and productive way to pass the time while traveling from city to town to city. Bruce even copyrighted a song or two of his.

I continued to write lyrics until his illness. While researching my photos and notebooks for these notebooks, I found several of them. But I never forgot how I felt when that teacher used his words out of context to us, who loved playing guitars and making music. I also never forgot what it felt like to be on the highway, windows down, hair blowing, writing songs together, and laughing. That magic highway where there were no problems, where no time passed, only joy, living life, freedom, love, and music, and rolling the windows down.

Marcus and I were becoming closer throughout the summer and the next school year, and in 1970 I was sixteen when Marcus and I ended up going out on our first real date. By that time, Marcus was nineteen and had started college. My mom's instincts told her to be cautious of this boyfriend. She was not going to let this guy take away my future and my dreams because she knew I was going places and would not be sticking around to live my entire life in this one place. She told me that I had a light, that something, that presence, and she knew I was different. But it was me who never wanted to leave to go to college somewhere far away so my mom wouldn't be alone. I felt that it wouldn't be fair to her for me to leave since the other two kids were gone, too. It made me giggle with delight when she told us that once we were all eighteen, she was going to move five hundred miles away from all of us kids.

High School Senior Photo 1972

Marcus went to a college in Kentucky called Bellarmine University, and I attended Indiana University, which had a satellite campus near my hometown. One day, out of the blue, he asked me to attend his church. I was not a member of any religion at the time. I was raised by an Episcopal mother and a Jewish father, so we celebrated holidays like Easter and Christmas with a touch of Hanukkah at the Christmas holidays, and we all loved it, but we were never regular churchgoers or a religious family. So, I told Marcus, yes, I would like that because most of my high school friends went there. It was St. Mary's, a beautiful church in a rural wooded area on a hill, with a welcoming, kind priest and sisters. Marcus and I made close friends with Sister

Marian and Sister Angela through music. We put together a four-person group, calling ourselves The God Squad, to play at early afternoon mass on Saturdays. Marcus and I were on guitar; one of the sisters was also on guitar, and the other was on acoustic stand-up bass. We performed songs like (Come On People Now) Get Together, Turn, Turn, Turn, Turn, Today While the Blossoms Still Cling to the Vine and other folk songs we loved that were appropriate for the church. Our harmonies were amazing and the instruments were perfect. Everyone welcomed our music, and the masses were filled up on those Saturdays. Marcus and I spent lots of time with Sisters Marian and Angela and loved our time with them. It was a good thing for us.

I discovered that Marcus was very controlling, and that's something I knew nothing about at that age and time. He was very mentally and physically abusive, as I saw it in the way he treated his mother, but I just didn't understand. It was nothing I had ever seen or dealt with in my young years. No one had ever treated me that way; I was always spoken to and treated well by family members. And as a seventeen-year-old, without ever being in that situation or witnessing it, I didn't know what it meant. It's no surprise that it meant that same controlling behavior for me several years later.

There were little things like a pinch on my arm if he thought I was going to say something he didn't like in front of his family. I had no idea why he wanted to control everything I said and did. One afternoon, we were all sitting in his family's living room, and I was going to jump in and comment on a joke he had told me earlier. He had no idea what I was going to say, but as I began to speak, he pinched my upper arm so hard that it left a bruise. I had no idea how to manage this or what to think. In my mind, it was all very confusing. I wonder what look I had on my face. I know I felt my face get very hot, almost to a sweat. I said nothing.

I loved his mother and dad and his siblings and wanted everything to be better. He had two sisters and two brothers. Marcus was the oldest of five. I have no idea why he needed to be so controlling; he just did. One scene I remember clearly from my teen years happened when we were at his house for some reason or another on a summer afternoon. His sisters and one of his brothers were home. He had a brother who was blind; I'll call him Riley (not his real name), Riley had Scarlet Fever as a baby, and it left him blind. Marcus's mom had picked up Riley from the school he attended, where he was learning not only the usual education all kids learn but also how to live as a blind person in a visual world as he grew into an adult. Marcus took great care of Riley and protected him from the world.

On this otherwise, uneventful afternoon, while Marcus, Riley, and I were in the living room, his mother was in the kitchen washing and putting away dishes, pots, and pans and getting ready to make dinner for her family. Hearing the usual clanking of pots and pans going into and out of the cupboards, something that seemed completely normal to me, it was obvious that she was making way too much noise for Marcus. He bellowed at her from the living room something like MOM, STOP! Then he completely changed into a raging, red-faced lunatic and stormed into the kitchen to let her have it with awful and harsh words. His words to her were nothing I could imagine ever saying to anyone, much less my mom. I followed from a distance to see what was happening. Her face lost all color and became ashen. Afterward, that same gentle face turned so blood red it was like a burning fire, and she didn't utter one word. She was, from head to toe and her heart, immersed in embarrassment because I had witnessed this action. But it was clear to me that this had happened before. I was frozen, not knowing what to do.

It was shocking that anyone could speak to their mother like that. It was very strange to me, but I felt like I couldn't or shouldn't ask him why he spoke to her that way. I remember several times during those early years that I observed that same type of behavior towards his quiet and kind mother, and she always tried her best not to show emotion over it. His dad was extremely sweet and treated everyone with respect and kindness. The other kids were all very nice, normal youths and teenagers busy watching their favorite television shows, doing homework, and just being kids.

One year at Christmas, his dad gave his mother a beautiful necklace. She was very shy and somehow nervous about getting nice things. He asked her to open it, and she did but hardly acknowledged it. She wouldn't take it out of the jewelry box and set it aside. So, he knelt beside her and opened the box, tenderly kissed her on her cheek, and fastened the necklace around her. It was an extremely beautiful, shiny cross that she had been wanting. I will never forget how embarrassed she was to open that box, and I don't know why, but I do know she had a very tough time showing emotion. Her free-spirited side came out only once that I know of when we all went to another relative's baby shower, and only women were there. Now, that was a beautiful thing to witness.

I don't believe Marcus's dad was ever aware of how Marcus spoke to his mother and treated her when he wasn't there. And it was my first glimpse into domestic violence, even though I didn't know it or understand it at the time. It came from the oldest son and not from her husband, and I know now that this is not that uncommon. Marcus was over six feet tall and weighed a muscular athlete's weight. And he used his size to intimidate people sometimes, me included.

I still could not imagine being in that position. I just wanted to know why this was happening to his mother. In my family, we always talked to each other about everything, laughed with each other, and were always encouraged so our lofty dreams were not diminished or squashed. This was even more relevant as my mom raised us alone and decidedly loved doing it.

I hope his parents grew old together and were able to express their love without problems when Marcus left home. After that, I thought about it often, I still think about it.

Fortunately, at that time, it wasn't happening to me or anyone else besides his mother, at least that I was aware of. I have a feeling she never told her husband that this was happening, and I never asked or tried to figure it out. Looking back, I unquestionably should have talked to his mother and sisters. I imagine that being a teenager myself, I felt like it wasn't my place to say anything, and I wasn't able to completely comprehend or explain it.

My Senior Prom Night

I will always remember my senior prom with Marcus. I was seventeen and in the prom queen's court. The girls were supposed to dance one dance with a boy from the prom king's court. All of my friends were there and we had big smiles and were shining. I was so proud to wear my Crayola blue-green colored halter top floor-length dress and felt like royalty wearing it. My mom made that dress for me, and it was just perfect. It flowed and floated as I walked and twirled as I danced the night away. Each girl in the prom queen court dance was to choose a boy from the king's court and dance with him to a specific song. I chose to dance with my good friend Bobby Shaffer. He was wonderful and kind, and he still is to this day. We were good friends and in a lot of the same classes.

Marcus was not happy about that. I could see his face steaming like a cartoon character with puffs of steam coming from the top of his head, his ears, nose, and eyes. His eyes changed into glaring red flashing lights, and his fists started to clench on the table as he watched. After that dance, we went back to our respective tables. I knew Marcus well enough to see that he was about to explode, but he tightened his mouth and tried to smile and not make a scene as his chin dropped and his eyes became slits as they looked up without moving his chin. I just wanted to keep that feeling of floating above the floor in my beautiful blue dress for the rest of the night and not think about Marcus and his temper.

By the time the prom was over, everything was just fine again with Marcus, at least for that moment. He drove me home. We lived in an old house up on a hill where the driveway was long and a little steep. Marcus parked at a place that was flat, but not quite up to the house. It was dark and he wanted to make out. I was OK with that since we'd parked there many times and had a little make-out session before I went inside. That night was different. He had been planning this.

Everything started like usual, but he seemed to push himself tighter against me, and I didn't like it.

He said, "It's time!"

I felt myself tensing up and trying to squirm out of his grip as his hands were moving all over me; they were everywhere all at once. I didn't know what to do. What's going to happen to my dress, my hair? What's going to happen to me? I wasn't sure whether I was scared or just inexperienced and needed to follow along. I wasn't so naïve that I didn't understand or know what was going on, and unquestionably I wasn't ready for this, especially in a car. He started to untie the neck of my halter dress top and move to my neck, and I couldn't decide if he was a vampire or just chewing on my neck like I was a steak dinner. He kept moving all over me, and it felt like I was in a river, feverously attempting to push my way to the surface but kept getting pulled under. Even when I told him to wait or slow down, he never heard a word I said.

This was not fun; it was not gentle or sweet; it was rough and hurtful. When it was finally over, and I'm pretty sure this was only about fifteen or twenty minutes later, he said to me,

"Well, we did it. You've been screwed. You'll get better; we just need to practice a lot."

It was not a nice or romantic thing to say to me. In fact, it was downright harsh and thoughtless. I was still confused and blurry about what had just happened. And I thought, to myself, maybe HE should practice learning how to treat someone. There was no love language, no soft touches, no anything. As a seventeen-year-old girl, not quite a woman, like all teenage girls, I wanted love, holding hands, kisses on the cheek, nice words, soft touches, and all the aspects of what we feel as desire at that age. This wasn't it. When I think back now, I don't remember even holding hands, I only remember Marcus keeping his arm around my shoulder or grabbing my arm whenever we were around other people.

He told me to fix my dress, straighten myself, and put my shoes back on. Was he scolding me? I couldn't quite understand my thoughts. Was this normal? We were supposed to get married in a couple of years. He had given me a little diamond promise ring, so was this all normal, and was it always going to be like this? Am I supposed to feel like this?

When I finally got inside the house, I made a beeline to the bathroom to change clothes, and I saw the purplish bruise on my neck. Immediately, I thought that I better hide this. The next day, I wore a top with a high neckline and called my best friend to find out how to make it go away. But, of course, nothing worked. My sister heard me talking on the phone and called our mom in the room. I was so nervous and scared that I had let my mom and sister down when this wasn't ever something I wanted to happen, and it wasn't even my fault. I didn't tell them the whole story. I just couldn't; I didn't even know how to tell them or where to begin.

When everyone at school saw it, I realized that Marcus was marking his territory. I was so thankful that my mom had taken me to the doctor for birth control pills when she knew we were talking about getting married. It was nothing like the movies, of course, and what about all the love songs I loved to listen to and sing? Were all men like this? Was I just dreaming and wishing? Marcus was so proud of himself. Did he think that I should be proud of him, too?

My mom asked me if I would like to cut down the floor-length blue dress to make a summer halter dress. I said I did, but in my heart, I knew I would never wear it again.

Fortunately, life goes on, and time passes. Towards the fall, just a few months later, I focused on going to the university because it was expected of me, and I had two scholarships that paid for all of it, but mostly, I was preoccupied and intent on making music.

Marcus and I played together in coffee houses, garage get-togethers, parties, local clubs, and wherever else we could as a duo, and with the four-piece band we put together with a couple of younger friends, Perry and Mike, during college. My heart and soul were immersed in singing and playing.

I decided long before this that a lifetime of music was my destiny. It was all I ever thought about, all I needed, and everything else that ever happened never existed in my real world or meant much of anything. I just wanted to have others feel the emotions and joy from the music and want more of it. I wanted to sing and play instruments every second of the day.

Although I liked most of my university classes, the biggest surprise of all was that I loved chemistry. Who knew? My psychology and writing classes were exactly what I imagined they would be like, with no surprises and a whole lot of learning of things I liked, but it depended on who the instructor was. Isn't that the truth for all classes, no matter what age you are or what the class is?

French was something that I felt I might need some time in my life, and after several semesters of Latin in high school, where I loved the mythology and how words we use today originated from Latin, it was my language of choice. For French classes, I had a fantastic instructor the first year, but after that, I was in a more advanced section and was disappointed that all we did was read French literature. We didn't learn much about speaking, writing, and communicating in the language. Philosophy classes seemed ridiculous to me. I understood the point of the class but disliked that it was about opinions, and the instructor prided himself on getting students to argue in an unstructured way.

I wanted college to be over so I could get on with my life. When I look back, it did go quickly, and so many things happened during that time. That's what college is for – making new friends, finding new ideas, becoming an adult, and making life plans. I still couldn't shake the feeling of restlessness.

During the summers, I lifeguarded and taught swimming so I could be out in the sun and help kids learn to swim. The rest of the summer days were spent playing guitars, singing, and working with my current band.

When I was almost done with college, I did what I always had done. I devised a plan for myself and made it happen. Marcus was part of that plan for now, although I would have done the same thing without him, and he knew that. He was treating me well, and I didn't foresee any issues, so in the summer of my third year in college at nineteen, almost twenty, I did something I never thought I would ever do – I married him just like he predicted when we were in high school.

Once again, my mom made my dress, and we were able to make all the bridesmaid dresses together. We had so much fun making the dresses, but I could feel that Mom wasn't thrilled with my choice of marriage at this time in my life. We went to look at fabric and pattern books. I found the most perfect pattern... A 1970s floor-length dress with long bell sleeves. The fabric was white with tiny little raised daisies, like a dotted Swiss fabric. I loved it. My bridesmaids and groomsmen all wore a different color of the rainbow blue, violet, green, pink, and yellow. The dresses were just like mine except in those same rainbow colors. The groomsmen wore 70s-style tuxedo ruffled shirts in each of those colors to match the bridesmaids with a grey tux. Color My World was my walk-down-the-aisle song and We've Only Just Begun for the walk back. I loved everything and every second. My flowers were white daisies and babies' breath, the perfect 70s look.

When it was over and it was time to move in with Marcus in the duplex he had rented previously. We found the place to be cute and small, but I liked it. This was when I discovered I liked having my own space, but it felt very crowded when Marcus was there. Eventually, I got used to it, and we moved to a single-family house in a more rural area, closer to my best friends. That was better. We could set up band equipment in the house and rehearse, or I could just be alone singing and playing Elton John songs on my keyboards. Marcus wanted to keep playing music, too, and he let me take the lead in putting the band together and choosing songs.

Starting with our four-piece band including Mike and Perry, we called ourselves Duncan Hill. Duncan Hill was a place in our area where train tracks went through. There was a sign on that hill, by the train tracks that read Duncan Hill. We liked the name so we tried it out. Later, as a group, we decided on a different band name.

We secured a great practice space and rented it. It was a big space where we added a nice-sized stage and painted the entire side wall black with the name Wildfire in white. There was another room that we made into a kitchen/breakroom with a small refrigerator, and a table and chairs since we spent all our time there. We added a backup singer and a new drummer since some of the first band members left to pursue more brass-centered and jazz music in the style of the group Chicago. We were there almost twenty-four/seven because it was so magical at that time. I still see the space clearly in my mind's eye. It felt good.

The goal was to get the band out on the road in the Spring of 1976. This was in 1975, and I had less than a year to get it done. I had no inkling of what was involved in how to do it, and there was no Google, no internet of any kind, or other place to look it up. However, that never stopped me from doing anything I wanted to do, I was just going to make it up and learn as I went forward.

Sadly, our first experience with theft happened at our wonderful practice space. The guys had a lot of tools there since they had built a stage and were building shelves to make the space more conducive to a home away from home. Too many of the band's friends and previous band members knew about this place. And even though it was always padlocked and in a building with other spaces for businesses, the friends of those guys broke in. The tools were stolen, but none of the music equipment because there were no guitars or other pieces of small equipment there, and the drummer had taken his drums home to practice. My keyboards were too big and heavy to grab. So, I'd say we got lucky. We found out from one of our good friends that the thieves were some cohorts of one of our old bandmates. We got our stuff back and put heavier padlocks on the door, but it never felt the same. The previous bandmate knew nothing about the robbery by his friends but felt like it was his fault because he had told his friends about our cherished practice space. I agree.

After deciding to get ourselves on the road and making somewhat of a strategy to get this all figured out, I realized that I had no idea how it worked and what the steps were. Remember, there were no computers or cell phones in the 1970s, so I needed to do some detective work. I wished that I had Maxwell Smart's shoe phone and Napoleon Solo and Illya Kuryakin's Man From U.N.C.L.E. high-tech spy equipment from 1966, so instead, I did the next best thing. I got the best technology at the time, a big fat phone book, and contacted local Louisville entertainment and talent agencies to come hear us and start booking us. That gigantic phone book was very high-tech for the mid-70s.

Lo and behold, the largest local Louisville talent agency, Triangle Talent, was the first to come and audition us at our Wildfire practice space and decided to give us a shot and send us out on the road. Where we lived in southern Indiana, Louisville, Kentucky, was just five miles across the bridge over the Ohio River. The area is called Kentuckiana.

Getting Started

I said yes to Triangle Talent because I was going to do it with the current band or not, and Marcus was not happy about quitting his good administrative job. But we were doing what we both knew was the very thing we wanted to do. Yes, he, without a doubt, wanted to do this with me. When I look at it now, I'm sure it was because he was fearful that I would leave on my own and never come back...I would have. Our equipment at that time was minimal, but it did the job. We had everything we needed to get out there.

The agency wanted to book us but also wanted to make some changes to the personnel in the band before going anywhere. The bass player and his wife, who was our backup singer, decided not to go since they had just been married. In my mind, I figured that would have been the best time to go, but they decided to stay. Some of the other early band members were not interested in hitting the road either and decided not to travel. That made the changes easy for the agency. We had Dan on the bass, his wife on backup vocals, and Bryan was our drummer.

Wildfire Circa 1975-76 photo public domain

The agency sent some musicians, and we wanted to hire back our first drummer, Perry, who we just loved, but he couldn't go out on the road at that time. The agency sent us a new guitar player, Barry (not his real name) which meant that Marcus would switch to bass, and I was on lead vocals and keyboards as usual.

We put some great songs together, and we were in but had no idea what we were doing so we kept on going. It didn't take long to find out. We had to have four hours of music to be able to cover three to four sets, forty-five minutes long, for five and six nights a week. That's what we did and have done ever since. At first, we had to choose more songs to do since most gigs we had played locally were two or three sets. Our first road set lists consisted of Fleetwood Mac, Ambrosia, Linda Ronstadt, Rubicon, Captain and Tennille, Elton John, KC and the Sunshine Band, Olivia Newton-John, Billy Joel, Little River Band, lots more, and oh yes, Feelings by Morris Albert and some disco.

Marcus, Barry, Perry and me 1976
photo public domain

My friend Vickie and I went shopping to find classier stage clothes. She decided that she could make a few things for me since she was a seamstress. We hit the fabric stores and the pattern books. She knew how soon we were leaving and was able to get several disco-type dresses made for me quickly.

Even though we were shaking our heads about how to put this all into motion, we did it. There were so many things to think about. Do I pack one bag or two? Do I bring everything or just a couple of outfits? What will I discover? I didn't know how to do any of this, but I discovered that this was a long-term lifestyle, and you don't go home after work because you're in a hotel in another state, and you play on holidays. We were booked fifty weeks a year as time moved forward. I loved it all, every single bit of it, the good and the bad, the unorganized packing, and figuring out everything.

Starting out, we had to drive lots of miles until we had an established route mapped out of venues we played on a rotation. We started in Kentucky, then drove to Florida, then back up to Virginia. Makes my head spin just thinking about it. Good thing gasoline was only around thirty-six cents a gallon. We also went to Minnesota, Wisconsin, Illinois, and Canada. By this time, GMA (Good Music Agency) in Minneapolis and an agency in Appleton, Wisconsin, picked us up. Drives were getting shorter, gigs were getting better, and so were we.

Playing music full-time, traveling on the road, living in hotels, and going wherever the booking agents sent us wasn't scary or the least bit unnerving for me. It wasn't stressful, it was superb, exciting. It was magnificent and I loved living this life just like I imagined it. Even with the puzzles and minor roadblocks, it was wonderful, and I never saw an end to it. I was twenty-two and doing exactly what I craved most in this world and learning more every day, entertaining people all over the USA, and doing it well, making myself a name.

Headshot Live Music Circa 1976

At first, I left, just taking some clothes, make-up, and the things you would need to stay for a week or two in a hotel, and our equipment. It was a cold February in 1977. The agencies and management immediately booked us for the entire year, fifty weeks a year, playing hundreds of miles all over the USA and Canada. Reality sunk in that if this is how it was going to be, we absolutely must be better prepared for driving hundreds of miles each week and living in hotels and vans. More clothes and more of whatever made it feel like home. In my heart and soul, this was an exciting job, not a big party and not a temporary thing. I became a little too comfortable living in hotel rooms because it was so easy.

I went from a suitcase or two, a makeup bag, and anything else a person might bring along for an extended vacation to larger trunks, travel cases, and things you need to live in a home away from home. After leaving some of my favorite clothes that I had put away in the drawers of some hotel furniture dressers in the first couple of hotels we were in, I determined that I had better do something different.

It was devastating because a stack of my favorite tops and T-shirts was missing. I discovered this setback as we unpacked at the next hotel hundreds of miles away.

I held back the tears when I couldn't find my cherished white Fleetwood Mac T-shirt with the cover of the Rumors album on the front. Marcus said that we should call the previous hotel to see if they could send it to me. That's what I did, but I was told that the room had been cleaned, and someone else had stayed there since we left. None of my precious cargo was found in that entire hotel, or so they told me. I get that same gutted feeling every time I think about it.

Eventually, all the suitcases and trunks stayed full, and the hotel room drawers stayed empty. Not unpacking was a perfect solution. Funny, but I still have some of this same mentality today, and not just when traveling but in my own home. Some might call it OCD (Obsessive Compulsive Disorder), like a fear of forgetting, losing, or misplacing something. I agree and admit to the OCD part. Maybe it's just a habit. After all the years of wishing I could wear that shirt, then finally forgetting about it, almost thirty-eight years after losing it, I finally got a new Fleetwood Mac Rumors T-shirt in February 2015 at The Dance concert in Des Moines, Iowa. It was so exciting to reclaim that same T-shirt, well, almost the same. The old one was a 70s-style white short-sleeved, more fitted women's T-shirt. The new one was black and had a loose-fit style. So what? I love it! And it was even more meaningful to get it at that specific concert since our set lists have always been full of Fleetwood Mac music since 1974.

Time moved ahead, and our main vehicle got bigger, as did the belongings we traveled with, which were also growing in abundance. We filled our box truck and band van with everything we thought we would need, from dumbbells to microwaves, small refrigerators, hot plates, pets, you name it, we traveled with it. I even had a small sewing machine so I could create my very own stage clothes.

During all the years of traveling, packing up, then unloading, and setting up our hotel rooms and the stage equipment, everything had to be just right for me in my surroundings. With no uncertainty, I felt that it was because I just wanted to be sure I could find everything each time it was moved. But it looked like I was the only one who was rigorously setting up my hotel rooms exactly the same way each time.

Someone in the band once asked me, "Why does that matter?"

I only had one answer...so I know where everything is. This still happens today. I absolutely must pack my music equipment the same way every time, and I become agitated when someone else does it differently and puts something in the wrong bag or case. But honestly, they just didn't get it, and it was not important to anyone else. The truth is, it saves time setting up and I know immediately if something is missing.

As you might expect, if you know me, I traveled with some dumbbells and a couple of other small pieces of exercise equipment that I used every night after the shows. When VCRs showed up on the technology scene, I recorded television shows to watch while I did my thing after the show every night. Besides the sewing machine, I carried a plastic tub full of everything I needed to create my own jewelry and clothing designs.

I had creative accessories and tools with me, too. I made a lot of jewelry and some of my favorite stage clothes from magazine pictures. Later, I got requests from other women we met in other traveling bands to make some jewelry or clothing for them in my designs and their choice of colors. I only did that a few times. The best time to use these skills handed down to me by my mom was when two of our fans from Texarkana were planning to get married circa 1986. They met at one of our shows and decided to make it forever. The bride wanted me to make her dress in a combination of royal sapphire and ice blue and a Western-style hat with draped pearls, and make the same dress in a smaller size for her ten-year-old daughter. It took up a lot of my time, but it was undeniably a lot of fun to create, and they looked beautiful in those dresses.

Texarkana wedding dresses Circa 1986

Some of the band members quickly came and went after playing for a month or two, not realizing this was, in fact, our new home. The agents and managers sent new musicians for us to audition. Some were fine, and some were less than ok, but until we had what I considered a mutual musical friendship and respectful situation, oh and yes, an agreement that this was our job twenty-four/seven, that's when it would start to work.

The members changed, with different drummers and bass guitar players and a variety of personalities and opinions. How we all interacted as people and as musicians working together was the only way to know if we would be comfortable playing together and if the music would be the best we could produce.

It was wonderful every time we started down that highway in our caravan, and it was a great way to see the country. Every type of scenery, with monuments, a thousand billboards, amusement parks, stores, shopping centers, and meeting so many new people made touring spectacular and thrilling. Many times, we would pack and load up so we could drive overnight in the wee hours of the morning to get to the next gig. We'd get there, check into our rooms, and set up our equipment the following day, which was usually Sunday. That gave us some time to relax and explore the new town. This was something we did until leaving the road life in the 1990s. Getting recognized at grocery stores and around towns, even with no makeup and dressed in jeans, was exciting.

My mom, who was always my biggest supporter, no matter what, never once let me know how terrifying this was for her. I only felt and heard her love and support. She forwarded my mail to each hotel or band house weekly, and I called her on the hotel room phones because, remember, there were no cell phones or email. When we arrived at our destination and a couple of times during each week. If only we would have had cell phones at that time because the hotel telephone bills were outrageous. And it was just as much of me checking in on her as it was to let her know I was ok.

Chapter 3 – The Early Days

Agents and Bandmates and Thieves, Oh My

Getting started and before leaving to tour full-time, we were hoping that our first drummer, Perry, a close friend and dynamic drummer and vocalist, would join us. He was extremely talented and fun to make music with, and he was a natural comedian who kept us all laughing. Perry could kick out anything on the drums at the ripe young age of fourteen when we put our first band together. During his junior high and high school years, he studied the style of Neil Peart for hours after school and developed his own solid, dynamic style. He was a fantastic singer, and we did several duets together. Perry and another band member in our local group left to do something different with their music after a couple of years playing around the Southern Indiana/Louisville, Kentucky area. So, we had to regroup. This was around the time that Marcus was on guitar, and his brother, Dan, who was possibly the sweetest but shyest person I have ever met and a joy to be around, joined us on bass with his wife on backup vocals.

Our drummer, Bryan, was a decent drummer and enjoyed playing locally. He had a few fire tricks he loved to do with his drum mallets. Yes, real fire. Unfortunately, even though they were impressive tricks, and nothing was ever damaged, none of the places we played, and probably would ever play, allowed him to do the fire tricks. Was there ever any doubt? Neither Dan nor Bryan wanted to travel, which was a positive thing that allowed us to progress.

Once we contacted Triangle Talent, they were more than eager to get us a new drummer and guitarist. So that meant Marcus would switch to bass. I remember our first road drummer, Tommy, because he was just so funny, a great powerhouse drummer who was always smiling with a big toothy feel-good laugh that rivaled Dom DeLuise and looked like his doppelganger. We played our first few road jobs with Tommy. He had no agenda, no bad days, and a sunny attitude. I loved singing duets with him and how his ease, flow, and style made the music work. Barry (not his real name) was our guitarist sent from Triangle Talent. A smooth, clean guitar player who loved Steeley Dan style. He had his girlfriend, Angie (not her real name) with him.

The first drive was to Bardstown, Kentucky. It was exciting and fun. On the way there, we anticipated what the gig would be like. It was a week in a popular, large club and filled up every night Monday through Saturday, with an eager audience. We spent our afternoons rehearsing to tighten up our sound and learn new songs.

As a woman on stage, I had been heckled at a few gigs, but the one thing I remember most about this incident is when some guy in the audience yelled out that he wanted to take me home to his mother. I looked in his direction and spoke into the microphone,

"I ain't the kind you take home to mother."

That was the last I heard from that guy, and the audience had a great laugh.

Our next journey was to the Brown Derby in Gainesville, Florida. It was glorious, sunny, and tropical in early March of 1977. We made this our home for two weeks and could not have been happier.

The Brown Derby Gainesville, Florida Circa 1977

During those two weeks, Tommy met a beautiful tall, blonde girl with a lovely personality, and they became inseparable. They constantly laughed and talked, held hands, and truly enjoyed being together. She decided to come with him on the road. After a couple of months, or maybe it was only weeks, they left to get married. I hope it worked out for them since it was such a whirlwind romance. But we needed to replace our drummer immediately with no break in bookings.

This time we were solidly focused on getting Perry back to play drums. It all worked out this time because he had missed playing with us too. Our agency was all for it, and we asked Perry to meet us in another city in Kentucky where we were headed next. He hesitated at first because he had a girlfriend who didn't want him to go and leave her at home. Relationships with musicians, especially traveling ones, are terribly complicated and seem selfish to the partner. However, those relationships can also work out sometimes. So, Perry and his girlfriend got their parents' blessings and married before coming out on the road. She and I were already friends, which made it great for us, and we were all happy for them and for the band.

We moved around from city to city, state to state, with Perry and his wife, our guitarist, Barry and his girlfriend, Marcus, and me. Tallahassee was next. It was a beautiful city and we met other traveling musicians there who were staying in the same hotel. I made good friends with a band from Florida and Alabama. The guitar player and I connected on a few different levels and ended up keeping in touch through cards and letters for a couple of years until he had a bad auto accident and had to go back to his home in another Florida city. He eventually married the woman who was his girlfriend and longtime caregiver after his accident. We spoke on the phone several times, but I didn't think that was a good idea. Marcus was already not happy that we had become friends and were communicating. I get that. That handsome, talented guitar player and I had our heart song. There is a song for every part of your life story. And when I heard that song on a 1977 countdown, it took me back to those exact moments. I went back to Florida several times while on the road with other band configurations over the years and it was always so beautiful. The way of life in Florida is easygoing and trance-inducing.

Throughout Virginia, Kentucky, Ohio, Tennessee, Kings Dominion Theme Park, King's Island Theme Park, Alabama, and Florida beaches, with lots of great music and fun together, Perry stayed on the road as long as he could until that common theme happened again. His wife wanted to settle down and start a family. They stayed with us for quite a while, even after they decided to go home.

Meridian, MS Circa 1977

Perry and I remained lifelong friends and frequently caught up with what was happening in each other's lives. He remarried many years later after leaving, moved to Alabama, and was extremely happy with his big extended family. Unfortunately, Perry passed away in the summer of 2020 from cancer. He didn't let many people know he was even sick, so this came as a surprise to me. He'll always be at the top of the ladder of family and friends in my life. Thanks, Magicman (his nickname), for all the music, memories, friendship, and fun. I feel your presence many times during each year.

Perry in Gadsden, Alabama circa 1977

Shannon hanging with Perry in Gadsden, Alabama circa 1977

Our guitarist at that time, Barry, was laid back and easy to work with, and, as I mentioned earlier, he had his girlfriend with him. We didn't know either of them before leaving to travel, but it all seemed to work out fine. That is, until she, Perry's wife, and I all spent a lot of time together talking. She was not having her best life living in hotels and wanted to go home to set up housekeeping and eventually marry. It wasn't long before Barry agreed and off they went. I sense a pattern evolving here. He was a good fit for the band while he was with us. He was no slouch on the guitar, and we were sad to see him go. The most memorable thing about his departure was returning to Indiana for the holidays that year. I called Barry and Angie to say hello and see how they were doing. Angie answered the phone. I told her who it was that was calling, and she replied with a very cold answer that went something like this: My husband isn't home right now. I'll tell him you called. That struck me as odd as if she didn't even know me. Maybe she thought I wanted to invite him back into the band. I'll never know for sure, and I didn't take it personally, it was just so weird.

Now, don't get me wrong, I completely understand the need to have a home and stay in one place. I get it. This is why my mom put down our stakes in Indiana when we were teenagers. But there is so much to see, do, and live out there for anyone who will take advantage. As a child, I had lived and moved from town to town, city to city, state to state, and it was always new, always exciting. Not many folks have this type of inner desire, energy, and ambition or is it wanderlust? But why would anyone live in one place for their entire life? That would sort of be like never leaving your bedroom.

I couldn't see myself living and working in one place for too long, and especially for the rest of my life. I didn't have the need or yearning for children or a so-called normal family life. There are lots of us like that in this world, and it's nothing I ever regretted.

As the band members changed, Marcus stayed on bass. He felt that he was much better on the bass than lead guitar and liked it. And he liked the lifestyle in general, except for the driving.

As the Dan Fogelberg song says, "The audience was heavenly, but the traveling was hell."

Seriously, not all the traveling was bad or even hard. Some of the highways and roads were long and exhausting. Some were dangerous, as our heavy van slid on an icy, winding mountain pass, but most of it was interesting and fun, filled with multitudes of different scenery and people. The rhythm of the road was and still is very exhilarating and creative. The anticipation of where we're heading was constantly inspiring and motivating. I still love staying in hotels for days on end.

As I peruse my ancient photo albums and envelopes full of drugstore-developed photos, I don't even remember or recognize some of the people or some of the band members. But the ones who made the biggest impact I will not soon forget.

Not all musicians we hired through agencies were always a good match or even satisfactory players. Any musicians we might need to replace came from our agencies or word of mouth on the road. The only way to speak directly to us was for them to call whatever hotel we were living in at the time. Sometimes we were called by an agent or manager to let us know a new guy would be coming to the next gig to join us. Either way, some were potentially a great match, some not so much, but they all had to learn our music and sing harmonies easily so there was no break in our schedule.

Joe and Steve L. were next up. Joe on guitar, and Steve L. on drums. They were fun to work with but not the best musicians, and it was a little uncomfortable. Joe looked just like Tony Orlando and was a satisfactory singer who sang a couple of Tony Orlando songs, much to the delight of the audience. He was fun on stage, which was important for keeping the audience listening and watching. Steve L. was an average drummer with high energy and a better singer than Joe, but he didn't overshadow him.

Joe, Marcus, Steve L. and Me Circa 1978 Photo Public Domain

Early on, we spent many of our travels in South Dakota, Nebraska, Tennessee and Missouri. I don't remember exactly why the two of them, who were friends before they joined us, left, but it had something to do with Steve's ex-wife. Go figure. I don't remember ever feeling sad that they had to leave, and we were getting new players, even though they were decent guys. And no big stories accompany them except that they were a blip on the radar.

It is a revolving door until you hit the right chemistry among all the players. Lots of egos are involved. Our next guitar player was Blair (not his real name). He looked like a California beach boy and seemed to fit in well at that time. Blair was from Alabama. He had a fantastic singing voice, played skillfully and smoothly, and his personality worked harmoniously with ours. Nonetheless, he had two major issues involving women that were not a very good fit. One was his longtime girlfriend, Hilary (not her real name), and the second was a girl he picked up on the road in Illinois, who I will call Katie. Katie started traveling with him, much to the chagrin of Hilary who didn't know until later and who kept close tabs on him. Hilary drove a lot to see us and be with Blair.

I liked Hilary a lot because she was so down to Earth and humorous. She was a lot of fun and comfortable to be around, very creative and happy, or so it seemed. Of course, she inevitably found out about the new young girlfriend. Katie's well-known father owned a chain of pizza restaurants throughout the Midwest, Florida, and other countries. I know you probably want to hear about a big chick fight between the two girlfriends, but stay with me, this is even better.

There was no female mud wrestling, but Katie's dad discovered that his daughter, who had been missing for several days, had run away with some musician. He didn't find out because Katie called and told him. She didn't. Since we were all over twenty-one, we thought she should contact her father to let him know she was safe. It was summer, and even though she was out of school for the summer months, she needed to tell her father that she would be home at some point. She did not even try to call him or contact him in any way. This was more serious than any one of us thought, and you guessed it, she had just turned seventeen years old and would be a senior in high school in the Fall. Her father called the police to report her missing and find out where his daughter was and who this guy was. And that, my friends, was literally the end of the road for Blair. He barely escaped being arrested, Katie was picked up and taken back home. Hilary, wisely, wouldn't take him back either. I have no idea what happened with all of them after that. But I bet Katie had a great story about her summer fling with the guitar player in a traveling band to tell her friends at school in the fall. You can't make this stuff up.

Next up were Sammy and John, a drummer and guitar/keyboard player who were also personal best friends. The two had played music together for many years. They were both extremely kind, thoughtful guys and expert musicians. They enjoyed playing any type of music and were both always smiling, calm, and very easy to get along with and had no egos. They were happy to sing and play any parts of any song perfectly and were creative and fun. Neither of them appeared to be partiers or womanizers. They stayed with us for quite a while until John became ill. We found out later from Sammy, after they left the band, that John had sleep apnea and had passed away. I'll always remember what fun it was to play music with them and their kindness not only to us but to each other. It was indeed a good chapter in all the madness of this road life, trying to find the ideal mix of musicians and personalities.

With Sammy and John circa 1978-79

You may be wondering how and why we just kept on going. It was because we were working with musicians who, like me, decided early on to make music their life work. And playing music on the road paid really well, as opposed to being a sideman in a well-known act. Almost every single person who worked with us was adept and good at what they did. We also knew that the right people just hadn't come along yet. It took a lot of overhauling throughout the years to finally make that happen. Eventually, it did, but not until the early 80s.

After Sammy and John, I fondly remember Steve T. and Harlan and their wives. They joined us as we played all over the upper Midwest. Steve sang and played some keyboards, and Harlan played drums. They were a pleasure to work with and had no control issues or a disruptive nature. Their significant others were lovely, dedicated young women who loved the music and their husbands but, as you might expect, soon tired of traveling. I don't blame them. It sounds like a glamorous life until you're doing it day after day, month after month. Not many wives, girlfriends, and significant others want to live this nightlife for long and watch other women ogle their partner, no matter how true he is to her. That lifestyle is a lot of work, although a great way to see the sights. However, living in hotels and moving everything you own from place to place every two or three weeks most of the year isn't the dream of most people if they had to choose, especially the women who love the men. Steve T. and Harlan stayed with us as long as possible, which was over a year.

This story happened while Steve and Harlan were in the band. Our guitar player in this arrangement of the band was Alan. Alan was an excellent player and singer and could write decent songs, but he was relatively quirky, OK, he was a lot quirky.

Alan picked up a girl while we were traveling. I know you've heard all of this before. This iteration may be a little different though. I don't remember where they met or what her given name was because she insisted on being called Chili. She had a thick head of red hair and felt that the name Chili made her somehow exotic and a firecracker. This girl really heated things up as she sat at the bars in the clubs every night of the week, hiking up her already short miniskirt and running up Alan's bar tab sky high. He must have given her a limit on spending because we would see her moving around the room finding men to solicit more drinks.

After four nights of this happening, the management at this place banned her from returning during our performances. She had to stay in the hotel room. Life on the road was always comical, always something new, sometimes ridiculous, and my psychology major came in handy daily.

While researching memories, I recently asked Steve T. and Harlan what they remember most about Alan. They told me the two things they remember most. First was his girl, Chili, well, who wouldn't remember that little hot pepper, and the second was the perpetual cricket noises he used to make. It was a habit, and he did it incessantly. They also remembered that Alan broke into one of the band vans and attempted to steal microphones at our last gig together. That's also the time I began seriously pondering the decision to leave and break it off with Marcus, which is coming later. I had forgotten about the theft, but it sure has come back to me now as Steve T. and Harlan tell it. That story made me laugh and shake my head. I suppose microphones are small enough to fit in a bag or pocket and he felt we owed him something. Thieves are common among band members who join for a short time and are usually fired and move on to the next group. It's

either a way to get back at the band or a souvenir of time spent, I suppose. Either way, it's downright contemptuous and despicable.

Harlan, Marcus. Alan, Steve T. and me Circa 1979 photo public domain

Marcus enjoyed playing and performing, and we had many good times throughout the years, but his actions were beginning to prove that he was tired of all the attention I was receiving, not only from agents and the audiences but essentially, from other men. He tried to stay calm and supportive. In other words, he tried to keep himself on a simmer, not a boil. But it was becoming an inherent danger to me as I saw him try to have an inner calm, which made him hold his breath and repress his temper, which, in turn, eventually made him explode with resentment, violent language, pushing, shoving, and asserting himself in my direction and always in private. Anyone who has experienced domestic violence will relate to this and the necessity to get out of the relationship and go far away.

After nine years together, six of those married, I was so exhausted from his controlling behavior and anger problems that I finally made the decision to tell him I was done and leave that potentially volatile situation. Playing music has always been my heart and soul. It made me complete. It was the joy and lightness of life, and I didn't want that to stop or dim because of someone trying to stomp me out.

I had endured unimaginable behavior from Marcus many times over the years we were together. Yes, it started back in college during those days before we left. Now it appeared that living out of a suitcase and a trunk was getting the best of him. Something I could understand because it seriously isn't for everyone. He could have just told me that he felt this way. But he had no idea how to do that and not lose me at the same time.

He was becoming more controlling and smothering, and he was starting to drink too much. It's a good thing that there were no cell phones, tracking devices, or other technology then. I only knew that I wanted to leave and not let him know where I was.

I never saw any of the money we were making. As a top-act band, we were well paid, on the high end of the scale, but I don't know for sure how much we were getting at that time since he collected the money, paid the agent commissions, and the other band members. He kept my portion of the pay because he wanted to be sure all the hotel bills were paid, including phone, food, and beverages. If I needed or wanted something, I had to ask. At that time in my life, I honestly didn't think much about it. That was just the way it was, and it was all about controlling me and everything I did. Most band members were unaware of this and found Marcus intense at times, but they generally liked him. Yes, he could be very likable, even to me sometimes.
There were those great times, the music, and the fantastic and fun places we saw and explored. We did have a lot of fun most of the time, but there were instances when he said or did things that confused me as to why, and it left me perplexed or just sad and mad.

For instance, I was driving our big band truck/van and had to stop for gas and check the oil in the vehicle. I pulled into a gas station, stopped the van, and before I could even open the door and get out to pop open the hood, it just happened. Marcus grabbed the back of my head and began continuously banging my head on the steering wheel and the dashboard of the van. There was zero provocation or words from me. I was completely stunned and terrified! Thank goodness there was no one else around. I know it doesn't make sense, and why would it? He had frequently been verbally abusive but rarely this physically abusive. But this was off the charts. I yelled STOP at the top of my lungs and asked what that was all about. Once he realized what he was doing, he stopped and said in a very scolding tone,

"I'm sorry, but you should have stopped earlier. What if the oil is so low we need to get something repaired?"

Then he began yelling at me about how stupid I was and again that we should have stopped earlier. It's a good thing I have high self-respect and common sense. I can't imagine how low my self-esteem would have become, which is precisely what he was going for. He said that he didn't want me to get a big head and think I was "all that important." No one in my family had ever spoken to another family member like that. Marcus was the only person I had ever seen treat anyone this way.

I knew I had so much more to do in my life. So, again, I developed a plan. As a side note, always have a plan before you leave an abusive relationship. This is the most crucial aspect of your decision in that potentially dangerous and violent situation.

I started to ask for my own separate room at all the hotels and told Marcus I needed this time to think. I believe he thought I would come running back to him since he was skeptical that I could even function on my own. We still played every night in cities and towns and on stages of all shapes and sizes. But I felt relieved when I could go into my own space afterward and lock the door. He didn't come knocking on my door or try to get to me in any other way because the other band members were always around. He remained civil to me for a time.

While working at a gig in Minneapolis, it felt like the time was right to make my move. I had been planning how to do this for months as I listened to Poco's song 'Crazy Love' repeatedly, so many times that it was helping to empower me. The lyrics go: "Tonight I'm gonna break away, just you wait and see." I knew what I was going to say to him. I would tell Marcus that I would be calling the agencies to tell them I needed to leave, why, and to find me a different working band. I didn't want to leave the road life that I loved, and I sure didn't want to stay in this absurd situation. There were always so many other music opportunities out there.

The day I broke the big news to him, I went to his room and knocked on the door. He let me in. I said I was done with this, and there was an eerie silence; he appeared to be confused. Then an immediate frenzy of his crying real tears. Then apologies and more tears. Next, a furor of his words pleading and asking me for forgiveness, but still telling me I was stupid to leave and I would never survive on my own, then one big right hook to my jaw that I didn't see coming. It was so fast like a colossal flashbulb exploded. Something that I probably should have been expecting but wasn't. I purposely didn't get up. I just stayed down on the floor waiting. I knew the cool-down period was coming. When I was certain things were a little calmer, I quietly got up, opened the hotel room door, and left without looking back or saying anything. He never thought I would literally just walk away.

The next day, I called the agents to tell each of them about my situation and asked them to find me in another group because I was done with this one. For the remainder of the contract, Marcus was civilized but ready to boil over inside like a simmering volcano. I had previously made friends with the band that would be playing there after our contracted weeks were over. They were closer locally and came to our last night there. A few of the members got up to play some songs with us. "Déjà vu" by Dionne Warwick and "Brass in Pocket" by the Pretenders are the tunes I can remember most clearly that we played and sang together with the other band. I have that scene in my head anytime I hear those songs to this day. I love the songs, and it's a good, happy memory of being on a big stage in front of so many people. Even though I was leaving and would be playing with other musicians, I knew I would stay in touch with some of those faithful audience members.

Marcus was a full-fledged narcissist. Narcissists believe whatever they do or happens is someone else's fault. They need to control every situation and everyone around them. Marcus felt this was all my fault. My mom, who was thrilled that I was leaving that mess, explained to me that some men are afraid of or feel threatened by strong women or women who are in charge of things like groups of people, job sites, offices, and just in general, and are puzzled, rattled making them feel that they have to compete with the peace and happiness women feel with their own solitude. Yes, women can be and, most times, are very happy on their own. However, in this case, it's the old philosophy of 'if I can't have you, no one can, I own you' or that someone or something is going to take this person away from him. I followed my instincts once again and got away from it.

Eventually, I discovered that while we were playing at the Minneapolis gig, Marcus had started seeing a young woman who came to our shows regularly after he knew I was leaving. I was not too surprised, and at the same time, it truly made no sense to me. But I was just fine with that situation because it meant he would leave me alone, and I hoped things would not be so bad for her after some time together. Years later, I learned that they had married and moved away to another northern Minnesota town.

After that last night, I went to my mom's house in Indiana just as she was getting ready to move to Houston, a decision she made sometime before all of this. A fast divorce happened for me, and it was pretty much the easiest thing I had ever done. Marcus didn't plan to show up. I didn't want anything he had, and there was no need for a court trial or anything like that. Just my mom's attorney. I didn't have to do anything. Done and done. I had my music equipment and everything I needed to move on. I was never in touch with him again, even though, over the years, I returned to Indiana, not only to perform but also for class reunions. Maybe I should have contacted his family when I was there, but I didn't feel that was a good idea. It was mostly because I never wanted him to know where I was.

Twenty-three years later, in 2003, I received a long apology email from Marcus. That's coming up in the chapter on Dangers.

There are so many stories and crazy, unimaginable things that happened along the way, which you will read about in other chapters. And yes, a lot of road band stories are very true.

CHAPTER 4 – SEX, DRUGS, LOVE, AND ROCK AND ROLL

It's Not In the Job Description

In my life, I have never enjoyed alcoholic beverages. I've had them in the past, and the drink would sit on the table in front of me while I stirred and "nursed" it and never really drank it. Not because I knew about or thought about the hazards, but because I didn't like it, the smell, or the taste of it. As a teenager when all the kids were getting Boone's Farm and Mogen David, I knew they all wanted to try something different they thought would be fun, something everyone else was doing. Even when I tried to drink these, they tasted just awful to me. I didn't get it. I pretended to play along and handed the bottle back to the next person. I would see my friends being fun or funny, then just ridiculous, and it was not a good time for me to watch them acting weird, stumbling around, and some of them throwing up or falling asleep. It was supposed to be a good time, wasn't it? I didn't see the need to try and fit in for these screwball antics; I had so much more to do, even at that young age, and music was so much more interesting.

When I got older and left home, I had drinks offered to me, bought for me, and they sat there too. I drank a couple of them once and hated the feeling it gave me and how it tasted. It wasn't fun, and I could always taste the alcohol, so I didn't drink anymore. This was not anything important to me in any way whatsoever. I just got ice water with lemon and lime. Some people laughed because they thought I was drinking Vodka on the rocks.

As the musical of my life progressed, consumption of substances was a normal thing for everyone around me, and it wasn't just alcohol. I'm talking about any type of drug, swallowed, smoked, or otherwise. All I knew was that the way it made people act. It would cause people to change personalities, have vocal problems, forget things, feel regret, and it made some people just plain stupid. It was never different, and as I traveled and worked with more and more musicians, it happened to be the norm. Some musicians and artists believe it helps them be more creative. Yes, that's true for those who can't seem to get inside of themselves to find and shine that light. However, I didn't like the way it made some male friends and fellow musicians think it was OK to say or do things in my direction that I didn't think were OK. Shutting it down before it started was what I strived to do, but that didn't always work because, well, life.

I had my share of incidents including those times with Marcus and being teased, bullied, pushed, groped, and a year or so later watching as one band member tried to win the proverbial game of tug of war with me being the rope and the prize if only to wear the badge of honor as the victor with bragging rights of ownership of me. No wonder I seriously liked my alone time after the gig no matter how fantastic each night was, I felt so uncomfortable being a part of the after-party. It wasn't easy to find someone to just talk with. I loved the stage and the crowds, but I needed quiet afterward. My ears would be ringing from the sound, the amplifiers, the crowd, and the electricity of performing was my drug; that's how I got creative. It still works, and that feeling never fades away. I genuinely enjoyed being around people who were true friends whenever we were in their cities or towns.

For many people, this is how it starts, and that's how it sometimes ends. Drinking, drugs, substance abuse issues, parties, sex, and cheating. It's honestly not part of the job description, it just turns out that way. But musicians will be musicians, no matter how seriously they take their job. We are entertainers and people pleasers. We are cut from a different mold and need to be the best at what we do, and we desperately want the audience, and people in general, to appreciate that in one way or another. Some agents and managers thought it was a mandatory part of their commission that any women in the band(s) were a bartering tool, a sort of bonus commission.

Drugs were many times free for bands or cheap, and whether you wanted any of it or not, it was everywhere. Alcohol, for the most part, was not free at the bar or the club scene unless the management offered one or two free drinks for the night to the band because bands would drink them out of business if the drinks were all free. But no one, indeed, ever had to search for drugs, and offering substances to musicians is what many people do because they think it's what we all want. Some of them do take it as offered, and some don't. Getting an education in life is always a good thing.

My experience has taught me that some substance abusers have genius, creative brains who literally cannot quiet down their heads from the constant spinning, racing, and scribbling of numbers, music notes, loud noise, crowd noise, or whatever it is that renders them unable to just function in daily life. And I don't mean function as a normal person, I mean just function, period. All creative people have this to some extent. I figured out exactly what I needed to relax, and it wasn't a pill or a liquid. Some try to fit in because they believe that's what's expected. Some are constantly searching for something, but they have no idea what that something is, and they never seem to find it. I believe those are very lonely people. Alcohol and drugs are the way they self-medicate. Some use it only because it is expected of them, and those can be the most dangerous. And others don't use it at all. There were even singers I met along the way who used bronchial aid tablets from the drugstore instead of learning correct breath and singing techniques. That's an addiction, too.

PAUL – Give Me the Night

I met Paul in another Minnesota city some months before the big breakup with Marcus. He would come to hear us play, so we got to know each other, and we hit it off as friends. On our breaks between sets, I would sit with Paul and his friends. We made sure to keep in touch, so if we were close enough, he would drive to see the band.

After I finished the contract at that Minnesota club, which was not as tense and disturbing as I imagined it might become after telling Marcus I was out. That time seemed to go by quickly and smoothly, and I felt like I could finally take a deep breath.

Paul, who lived in an uptown area of the Twin Cities contacted me at the hotel we were in to catch up and see if we were playing anywhere near the Twin Cities soon, so he could come hear us. He was a genuinely nice, decent guy. We decided to meet in the Minneapolis suburb where he lived and worked. He didn't have an "agenda" that I could see and was just a polite guy from the Midwest. Once again, my instincts were right on. He was a kind, generous guy with a big heart.

I filled Paul in on what had recently happened and that I was waiting for a call from any of the agencies. He invited me to stay with him in his Hallmark-worthy charming, upscale apartment in that Minneapolis suburb. This was a guy who knew I would be leaving as soon as I heard from my management. Still, he said he would come to get me and my equipment.

This was quite a change from my current life. He took me dancing in beautiful clubs, to the best restaurants, and shopping and did not expect anything in return. He was always more than kind, gentle, and caring to me. Sounds like a tall tale, but it was true, and I finally felt comfortable knowing that this was the short break I needed. I didn't have to fight to stop him from grabbing and groping me, which, unfortunately, is something I had gotten used to from some men, whether or not I knew them. This felt good, like a one hundred percent real relationship. Paul showed me the difference between sexuality and sensuality. That was all new for me and eye-opening.

It was an amazing time to be in the brilliance of Minneapolis. The battle for the best of the best between Prince and Morris Day was going on, so downtown rocked every night. This was an incredibly exciting city to be a part of. The people, the lights, the music, the energy were all exactly like I had envisioned. It was big, it was luminous, electric, flashy, radiant, sparkling, and loud. I was able to go out on the town on a Saturday night to hear some entertainment and do some club hopping instead of being the entertainment and never getting to check out the city. I loved it for a short time but would rather always, for the remainder of my days, be the entertainment instead of in the audience.

Paul visiting me, circa 1980-81

During this time, my name was in the music gossip around town, and I was asked to play piano with a funk band named Haze until they got a permanent keyboardist. They are now known as the long-lost Minneapolis funk band "Haze". These men were such magnificent musicians, very respectful of me, and it was new for me to play this type of music. I love funk music. It was challenging and worth every second I spent learning their music on my Korg SG1 piano. At the same time, I was sought out to sing Pat Benatar-style music with a rock band from St. Paul, whose name I have forgotten. I worked with both bands temporarily, to my jubilation. I had lots of opportunities to do studio work over the earlier years, but these were the best with the best techs.

Concert Show in St. Paul 1980-81

I loved Minneapolis/St. Paul and lived in Paul's spacious condo in Edina, an affluent Twin Cities suburb where there were lots of things to see and do. The soundtracks of that time were Prince, Morris Day, and Journey's Infinity album, which I loved. Wheel in the Sky and Lights have always been my all-time favorite Journey songs, and I still love singing them. I still perform them today, and they always remind me of downtown Minneapolis in all its 1980s splendor.

About four months into my stay in Minneapolis, I received the call I was waiting for. A traveling band from Fargo/Grand Forks, North Dakota needed a female vocalist and a keyboard player. That was convenient for me since I could do both. I told Paul what was happening and that I would be leaving again. He knew nothing was going to keep me from my chosen life and profession, and he also knew I was not looking for a long-term relationship and to stay in one place, but I felt that he was. Knowing that I was going to take this new job with the new band, he was supportive and loving but apprehensive and a little sad.

We still had a surprisingly good long-distance relationship. On the weekends he drove anywhere I was performing, no matter how far away, whenever he could. We had a fantastic time exploring cities and towns and having fun together. Being apart more than together is just what happens in this situation. Since there were no cell phones or computer email, I vividly remember a time we were booked at a beautiful resort. The phones there had been out of service for a few days. Daily phone calls had been the routine for Paul and me, and the phone bills had been crazy, but this time there was no way to get in touch. We felt like our lifeline was gone. After that, I just knew it was time to discuss where this was going because, in my mind, it wasn't going anywhere. How could it when there was not an inkling in my mind about trying to settle down, and I was always fine on my own? No way was that in the cards for my life. We talked about it after the phone lines were back and knew we needed to figure it out in person.

There were a few more times we saw each other for a weekend. It didn't feel right in my heart. He made one more visit, and I decided it was time to end it. It wasn't a fair relationship for him, and I wasn't about to stop my life. When someone loves a traveling musician, no matter how much the musician loves them back, it's not easy. The one at home is alone most days and weeks of the year, and even though they stay faithful to that musician, it can't be reasonable to expect them to wait. Only being together for a few weekends or a couple of weeks throughout an entire year probably isn't what they signed up for, even though they might have known that all along.

We stayed friends and checked in with each other occasionally for about a year. He tried to come and visit a couple of times after that, but he finally realized that I was not going to allow that to happen. I'm pretty sure I broke his heart, and I would be lying if I said that I didn't shed a few tears over this relationship. It was the first time that had ever happened in any relationship in my life this far; real tears.

Once you live on the highways of freedom, stages, and spotlights, the last thing you want to do is stop it. Even a week or two off felt like an eternity, and I was ready to get out there again. It's addictive, electrifying, magnetizing, and mesmerizing, and you want to be with others who understand that and are also in it. Sharing that life with someone who is not in the business is unfair. But the memories are significant and lifelong.

His song for me.

"She was a friend to me when I needed one

Wasn't for her, I don't know what I'd done

She gave me back something that was missing in me

She coulda turned out to be almost anyone

Almost anyone With the possible exception

Of who I wanted her to be

Running into the midnight

With her clothes whipping in the wind

Reaching into the heart of the darkness For the tenderness within

Stumblin' into the lights of the city

And then back in the shadows again

Hanging onto the laughter

She wasn't much good at stickin' around, but

That girl could sing – She could sing

In the dead of night

She could shine a light

I will forever appreciate everything Paul did for me, all the things we did together, and the wonderful ways he brought happiness and calm into my life at just the perfect time. The excitement of experiencing the Minneapolis nightlife with him, hand in hand and in more ways than playing and singing while he was in the audience. Little did I know what was coming.

1981 The Late Show

The next chapter of my life blew wide open with independence, freedom from ties, and no one trying to control my life, or so I thought at the time, with the excitement of something new, and it brought even better and better music. Now, about this new gig, it has to do with possessiveness, abuse, new love, great music, and becoming a big name in the world of traveling musicians. I was thrilled to be an in-demand female singer and musician, but I was not thrilled to be a possession, property, or a staked claim.

The new group was a band from Fargo/Grand Forks, North Dakota. The male singer, Rob (not his real name), who was probably the biggest egomaniac I had ever met, immediately decided that I was his property. Here we go again, I thought. I didn't know that this would be part of my journey yet, so I joined that band from Fargo when my management told me this was what I should do for more exposure. This was with a new agent and another manager who wanted only my photo and face for the band photos. The boys in the band could have cared less, but Rob, who was the supposed band leader, wasn't thrilled. So, they set up the photo shoot for both of us and cropped his part out saying, "Sex sells, beautiful women sell, talented, beautiful women draw crowds." It was underhanded and tricky, and I had no idea that was going to happen, but to me, it was a funky situation, knowing that management always has the final say in publicity.

Headshot 1981 photo public domain

This band also needed a guitar player, and since I had several years of experience, that piece of the puzzle was going to be my job. I was told no one else likes to talk to agents or interview musicians on the phone. So I became the band leader again. It was the time when crossover country and pop music was all the rage. Urban Cowboy, Waylon and Willie, Dolly, Kenny Rogers, Crystal Gayle, Eddie Rabbit, Ronnie Milsap, Bonnie Tyler, Reba. I hope you remember all the music and magic of those times. Also, the time of Bob Seger, Laura Brannigan, Sheena Easton, a new style for my idol, Linda Ronstadt, and so much more to make this an incredible time to be a touring musician. Many of the big names were in the same cities and staying in the same hotels we were in, so running into them in the elevator or lobby, exchanging autographs, and making small talk about playing music and where we were from was not unusual.

In this group, we had a drummer, Lorence (not his real name) who was a great funky, solid drummer. He had played with Rob in the past, and they were friends.

This next part is important. Around 1978, I purchased a new camera to use on the road, and my sister sent me several new high-end filters that I could learn to use to practice photography. This camera was from about 1980 and was spectacular for the time. I had already taken several rolls of film that I wanted to develop, and I was waiting to be in a town for more than one week because that's how long it took to develop the film.

We were in the throes of a massive blizzard. I had taken several photos of ten-foot and higher snow drifts and other landscapes, as well as people, indoor pools, families, vases full of flowers, and other types of photos wherever else I could see beauty at all times of the year, even in the dead of Winter with thirty to eighty below-zero wind chill temperatures. It was a great creative hobby for me and so much better than my trusty Polaroid Swinger camera.

Lorence seemed to be an alright guy until Rob decided to fire him. I don't think I ever found out why. I surmised there was a disagreement about drugs or whatever they were doing. Drugs were a big part of that band. But on the day that he left, as we were packing up to move on to our next gig, I couldn't find my camera. I had always stored it under the bed in my hotel room or in the hotel room closet. It was nowhere to be found. I checked with the front desk to see if any of the housekeeping staff had seen it.

I told Rob, and he knew where to go right away. We drove past Lorence's car and stopped to look inside. There it was right on the front seat of his car, still in the soft leather camera case. We wouldn't break into his car to get it, so Rob went back to find him. Of course, he was nowhere to be found. I never saw that camera or the rolls of film again. I was heartbroken, to say the least. Rob was able to find out where he was and confronted him a few days later. I discovered that Lorence had asked the front desk for a key to my room pretending it was his room number, and they gave him a key. I suppose the desk figured we were all in the same group, so why not? Lorence knew I had that camera somewhere in my room even though he had never been in that room. He found it.

By then, he had sold it or pawned it. He told Rob that he had no idea about this camera, even though we had seen it in the seat of his car. I was so sad, and as time passed, I kind of forgot about it, but I never got over it because I still think about it and how many rolls of film I had taken that never got developed and the gift of different lenses and filters from my sister. I imagine it ended up in a pawn shop or traded to a dealer. I understand that he was an experienced thief, a drug user and dealer, and too close for comfort for me to be playing in the same band.

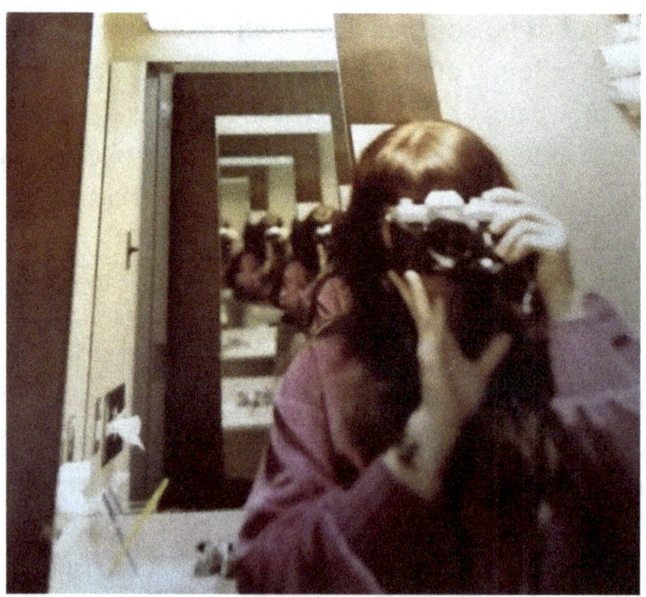

We reformed with a drummer named Mike and his brother, Gene, a fantastic singer and guitarist who played multiple instruments. The bass player was Jeff H., And then there was Rob, that male singer.

We traveled everywhere around the Northern and Midwestern United States and up into Canada. The audiences were spectacular, and Canada was beautiful. The pay was abundant, and I loved shopping in Winnipeg, Ontario, and other bigger Canadian cities. Everything was upscale and a lot like shopping in New York or Minneapolis. Besides, shopping was something I did with great enthusiasm.

These guys were all very kind and respectful to me, at least at first, which I greatly appreciated. We moved from place to place, as usual, and the band members were changing little by little. Gene and Mike left. Mike went home to his wife, but Gene went to Nashville and proceeded to win major accolades and awards as a sought-after Nashville guitarist and vocalist. He is on hundreds of recordings by major artists in Nashville and is still making that happen today. Gene is also happily married and loves his life. Mike went home and decided to stay there. They were fun and talented. I stayed friends with Gene and never heard much from Mike, but I am sure he's content at home with his family.

Gene, Rob, Jeff H., Mike and me Circa 1981

A new drummer joined—Richie (not his real name). He was a young, talented showman who absolutely looked like a rocker with long, wavy dark brown hair and a baby face. When he was performing, he put on a great show, standing up to play, twirling his drumsticks, singing some backup, and giving girls the eye. He undeniably had a presence. But I had a strange feeling about this kid. He would make derogatory comments behind us as we played. Not a great way to have band camaraderie.

The popularity of this band and the fact that girls wanted to be with Richie everywhere we went was not unusual. Richie was caught up in making sure he found a girl every night, which he did based on what I saw happening. He was a drug user and drinker. Sadly, he had some drug and alcohol-related issues, which led to health issues, indirectly and directly. Meaning passing STDs on to others. Right, nothing new. Some of those health issues caught up to him later when we noticed, while staying in a large, roomy band house, that he would turn up the volume on the television every time a commercial or update was on about herpes or other STD information. It was obvious to us why he did that. We shook our heads and made light of the situation, but there was nothing funny or light about it. It's just kind of creepy, especially when you consider all the women he had been with during the short amount of time I knew him, which was only a couple of years. I truly hope none of them contracted his affliction.

And there was Bill, a guitar player with talent and long fingernails he used as guitar picks. Bill appeared to be a good guy, friendly, a great player, and had a girlfriend who we never saw at gigs or anywhere else. Unfortunately, we discovered that Bill was not such a nice guy; he only posed as one in public. There was a lot of domestic violence in that relationship, and his girlfriend ended up with a broken nose and other injuries more than once during the time he was in the band. We saw photos of her which were horrific. I hope she left him and never looked back. We never saw her or talked to her because Bill controlled everything in her life. Rob told him his behavior towards her was not tolerated, and as long as he was in this band, he would not do anything to ruin our reputation or the reputations of the other band members. Nevertheless, Bill was allowed to stay in the band as long as he wanted. Later, I found out that it was a 'birds of a feather' situation. So much for that.

Bill was not much of a lead guitarist, although he was a fantastic rhythm player. We needed a lead guitarist. It was curious that I was put in charge of all the management, agencies, and hiring of musicians, just like previously. Rob disliked talking to managers and agents on the phone, and he also didn't care much about interviewing new musicians to hire.

That worked in my favor. We were under the management of a new agent, Ken Summers, and needed a lead guitar player who could also play multiple instruments since Bill was not very comfortable playing lead, and since I was the one in charge of hiring, Richie, our drummer, had mentioned someone that he worked with in another band and highly praised his talent. I got this guy on the phone (no cell phones yet. Still early 1981) and hired him immediately. That was Bruce and thus, the beginning of this story.

When I spoke to Bruce on the phone, I felt instinctively and positively that something different had just happened. We both had an immediate connection as if we had already known each other, even though we'd never met. I hired Bruce Breazeale from Iowa City just from that conversation. He had been playing with a couple of other well-known bands that were opening for big-name concert acts. It was an immediate soul mate experience, which was a new experience for both of us.

Our voices harmonized perfectly from the start without effort, it felt natural to us, just like breathing. Bruce played several instruments with natural ability: Lead guitar, pedal steel, fiddle, and keyboards. Playing music and singing with someone like that, someone who is a piece of your puzzle that you didn't know was missing, is a whole other level of spiritual relationship and making music. It's magical and surreal. I can't quite explain it, but everyone in the band and those who surrounded the band could feel it too.

Unfortunately, this caused some chaos among other band members, particularly that male singer, Rob. Bruce and I both knew there was something there, but it was a while before we got together, and I wasn't a fan of his drinking and drug use. I told him about my feelings on this subject. It made a minimal difference as he stopped using multi-colors of pills daily, at least. He indulged now and then. I wasn't a fan of anyone doing those things on such a regular basis, or ever.

As I mentioned, it was a little while before Bruce and I got together. We were all staying at a hotel close to our manager's house. His house was also his office. It was a big house with large rooms that could house a studio and various rooms so musicians could stay over and feel comfortable. Some members of his other bands were there as well for a get-together and to meet each other, which Ken organized regularly. Some would stay at the house as well. Ken loved having all his groups together and interacting with each other.

Some of these guys I met during this time were great friends, and I am still in touch with them to this day. I even worked with a couple of them in the early 2000s. Bruce and Jeff H. weren't there that Sunday evening, and I was hanging out at the house with a couple of other bands. Rob was off somewhere with one of his girlfriends. I called the hotel and asked if Bruce and Jeff H. wanted to join me at Ken's house. Jeff H. decided to stay at the hotel and Bruce came over. I knew why he came over, and I knew I wanted him to come over. I also know why Jeff H. didn't come with him even though Bruce and Jeff H. had become best friends. We sat on the sofa, and I will leave the rest up to your imagination because we weren't the only people in the room, even though it felt that way. When we returned to the hotel there was a group playing music in the lounge. We decided to dance to a slow song, and I don't remember what the song was, only that we blended and melted into each other. We were already becoming inseparable.

Jeff H. and Bruce Circa 1985

Jeff H and me Circa 1979-80

The boys in the band passed around not only drinks and drugs but also the women in every town and city who wanted to be a part of the whole scene. The drummer we were working with during this configuration of the band even set up his little sister with another guitar player while we were all in town. This wasn't unusual. For a lot of players, it was one of the reasons they were on the road, and many of those guys, of course, were married and had wives and/or kids at home. In their eyes, it had nothing to do with their families. It was an entirely unique and separate lifestyle. They felt no restraints and no obligations, almost like their alter ego was out on the road. It's a rude awakening when they return to the husband/father persona when they go home to find out that their kids have grown, as they wonder how all this time had passed so quickly.

Alcohol and drugs of all shapes, colors, and other substances were like three meals a day around a lot of the guys. I was not interested. But I saw how it changed the very course of their lives.

Regrettably, this happens way too often. Recently, and more than once, I've witnessed what a lifetime of someone knowing what they are doing and how this is eventually going to cause them future health problems but not taking steps to change those things to stay alive since that's the future and not affecting their now. These habits and actions will affect the people who love you and those surrounding you. This happened to more than one of the people I played music with.

Jeff H., the bass player in Rob's band, stayed friends with Bruce and me for a long time after we left that group. Jeff H. told me he loved me before we left. He tried to show me, but I never knew. He was one of the kindest people you'd ever want to know. He was considerate, talented, quiet, funny, and loveable but was consumed with alcohol. He tried to stop but couldn't stand the noise in his head and the shaking during his few attempts to detox. Bruce and I stayed close with Jeff H. throughout our years of traveling after leaving Rob's band. Jeff H. would visit to see Holiday Road Band when we were in his home state of North Dakota or even close by. He ultimately got off the road and stopped substance abuse, at least for a time. He married later in life but passed away from the abuse of his body and brain in 2011. This is how I watched Bruce get sick, get better, get sicker, and eventually pass away. And that was exactly what he was told would happen.

Bruce and Jeff H. Circa 1982

What if you sat down to consider your life so far? From the 1970s and 80s into the 90s, I have seen what the ravages of unhealthy lifestyles will do. I lived among musicians, fans, and groupies and witnessed "parties". I was not impressed by that lifestyle, and I wasn't the only one who was the odd person out. I didn't make fun of the others and I didn't complain to them about what they were doing until Bruce's habits got to be too much. I disapproved and protested more and more as it got worse with each passing year. Unfortunately, that never works. By the late 80s, I was exceedingly angry and sad that he was so self-destructive. He tried many times but was never able to make it stop for long.

Bruce had that constant frantic brain input, and the only way to slow the madness was one substance after another or being around a lot of people. That input also meant he would leave after the gigs some nights to hook up with a woman he met that night. Some nights I knew he was heading to an after-party, and though I wasn't too happy about it, that was the way of the world. Believe me when I say this was not part of the job description, but it was part of the lifestyle. He was a very kind, gentle soul, and alcohol didn't change that. But alcohol made him feel like he could function normally (whatever that is). He always seemed to be chasing something better and greater, but he never knew what it was. As the years passed, it was irreversible.

Not everyone followed the party-after-the-gig mentality. Inevitably, it stems from the need to wind down. It's like sitting down in front of the TV after a long day at work with whatever you need to wind down: a drink, junk food, or just some quiet. It just so happens that our after-work was 2 a.m. or later.

Instead of the extra noise and being around another crowd of people who had been drinking all night, some of us just wanted a quiet space to relax. And that's absolutely what I did since it made more sense and because I had things I wanted to do. I had solitude and quiet, and I could think and be creative. I didn't want to ruin my voice or my organs and shorten my own life. And I didn't want to sit and watch everyone else keep the party going until they passed out or worse. I had seen that plenty of times, but I was not in touch mentally with the things I witnessed. People were mainly just absurd, foolish, touchy-feely, obscene, and loud. Girls were there for the substances and to see if they could get the attention of a band member and, of course, it worked every time.

I started to think about what we were all breathing in every night for five and six nights weekly. I didn't want to inhale any more smoke of any kind after being in a smokey bar, club, concert hall, or other venue. The no smoking inside laws were not in effect in those years. And yes, everything always smelled like smoke: our instruments, clothing, hair, jewelry, all of it. What did our lungs look like? I don't even want to know. But it was standard at that time for all of us who spent so many hours a week in that environment.

Everyone was trying to hook up, no matter if they were already involved in a relationship or single. The band members were the people to hang out with after the show. It made all the clubgoers and fans feel important. I completely understand that. The girls and guys in the clubs and audiences were more than willing, as were the band members. Some (Bruce included) would head to the after-party at someone's house in towns we weren't familiar with or be invited to someone's hotel room after playing, coming back around 6 a.m. I didn't like it, but then again, I didn't stress about it much because I didn't want to know what they were doing and I was genuinely content going back to the hotel room for some quiet, doing my own thing while my ears were still ringing from the show, which was a nightly thing. That doesn't mean I was unsociable or a party pooper or anything else you want to call it. Remember, this was happening five and six nights a week. Going to bed at 3 a.m. meant getting up around 2 p.m. the next day. Some partied into the early morning until 5 or 6 a.m. Our days were on a different time frame.

There were nights when some actual fighting came about from clashing personalities, drugs, alcohol, and groupies. It could happen anytime, but mostly it was after the shows when energy was way up, and so were substance levels and tempers. It wasn't always like that. Between the calm and not-so-calm or rational discussions, the bloody, knockdown fight matches, and high emotions, it was the best of times; it was the time of our lives. When people live together twenty-four hours a day, seven days a week, especially creative people, things happen that can get out of hand, then cool back down again once everyone is finally more sober. But something else also happens; you become a family, and families are complicated.

I remember a night in 1977, another band was staying at the same hotel and playing at a different venue. We made friends with some of them earlier in the week. One night, from the deck of the hotel, I heard some thunderous yelling from a woman and a man. About thirty minutes later, one of the female vocalists from that band came pounding on my door to talk to me. I didn't know her, but I knew she was in the band staying in a different wing of the hotel. She wanted to know how to get her voice back from the shouting and screaming argument she was having. I helped her with a concoction of warm salt water, lemon, honey, crushed ginger, and cayenne pepper. I told her to sip it throughout the night and all day the next day. It worked. She also stayed quiet that next day and only spoke if she needed to, and no whispering, which is worse for her voice than speaking loudly. She went to the indoor pool in that hotel for a couple of hours that next day for the steam and humidity. She told me that the two of them made up and made a pact to stop drinking so much. Go figure. I hope, for their sake, that it worked, and I wish we would have crossed paths again. Later, in about 2010, I learned from one of my all-time favorite guys, singer/songwriter Richard Marx, that this was his vocal concoction, too.

One of the worst nights for me while in Rob's band goes something like this. I was in Grand Forks, North Dakota, at the apartment Rob kept in the city. He had invited a ton of fans and friends over. Of course, he wasn't there, so I ended up being the host. He was out with one of his female fans scoring more than drugs. I was there alone, which I preferred, just waiting for the deluge of fans and friends. In just a few minutes, people began pouring in and taking up every seat, the floor, and wherever they could plop themselves to fill up the living room. It felt like this had been going on for such a long time, and I just wanted to hide in another room, but only after a short time had passed once everyone had been there; suddenly, so much smoke had filled this place that I couldn't breathe. There was a thick fog from all the smokers, and I was choking, trying to get some air. I walked over to the windows and opened all of them, even though it was snowing and about thirty degrees with a nasty wind chill, a common occurrence in North Dakota. I told everyone to leave, and they knew I was serious, so they left, but in their own time.

I was reasonable and a little too nice about it, but I felt like I was having an asthma attack, and I had never suffered from asthma or allergies before in my twenty-six years. Finally, when they had all gone home, I kept the windows open for a couple more hours. This is where my battle with sinuses and allergies began. It was too much. All the years before this incident in smokey bars and halls had never affected me like this. This apartment was a smaller, enclosed place.

I started to become hoarse when speaking; however, singing was fine. It began to get worse. Since we were playing next in Iowa, I made an appointment with an ear, nose, and throat doctor at the University of Iowa Hospitals and Clinics. I found out I had developed nodes on my vocal cords. I was thankful that they weren't bad. This happened from all the stress of battling with Rob, the controlling self-appointed alpha male in this band, and putting myself in the position of fans and bandmates who were constantly smoking anything and everything.

I was relieved that the doctor said I should take three weeks off, take the antibiotics he prescribed, plus a short round of low-dose steroids, and I would be fine. So, Bruce and I headed to his parents' house in Iowa City for those three weeks. It was another case of perfect timing for physical and mental rest. I came back better than ever. Nothing like that has ever happened to me again, except for the lifelong, year-round allergies that I retained.

We felt it was time to move on from that mess. Bruce and I started to cultivate a plan to break out of that explosive scene of constant drama. We left that band in 1983 due to members with substance abuse issues and terrible fighting, the knockdown, bloody, drag-out kind, plus the mental and physical abuse.

When we told everyone after playing that night, the drummer, Richie, was high and drunk and started a street fight in the kitchen of the beautiful band house. Bruce and I had gone into our room, but soon the noise came. It all happened so fast, like a bullet train. Doors were pushed open, fists flying, and Bruce was dodging badly thrown drunk punches and trying to move out of the way but could only fight back as Richie followed him no matter where he went. I don't even know how long this lasted, but Bruce got a broken nose, Richie fell down the basement steps, and the magnificent Juno synthesizer keyboard I had just purchased and left on the kitchen table out of its case had landed on the floor. Blood spattered all over the walls of that kitchen. This is what happens when no one is listening and no one is thinking, just reacting. Everyone eventually ended up fine, even my keyboard.

We drove to an emergency room so they could take care of Bruce, and there's more to this story in the chapter on Dangers. No one called emergency 911 because there were drugs in some of the rooms of the house.

Our management was not too happy about the rumble in the band house roost, but they also knew we were on our way to better things by getting out of those completely erratic and insane circumstances and away from Rob's reputation, which was becoming significantly tainted around the country and in Canada. In the summer of 1983, we formed a new band with musicians who not only came and went but some who ended up being a big part of our family to this day.

Living and working with the same small group of people can be stressful and disturbing at times, especially when they are creative musicians who are doing road work because it's freedom and fun and lends itself to artistry, or not so much in some instances. And then there are those musicians who are looking for a 24/7 party experience, which is the downfall of so many talented players. Luckily, there were also those we worked with who respected me not only as a top-notch singer and musician but also as a leader, as well as the talents, abilities, and drive of the other players in the band who blended and wanted to stay with the lifestyle and the music. Not everyone who travels is a substance user, I am not, and many of the guys I made and make music with were not and are not. Making decisions about the professional musician's lifestyle is a personal one. However, so many don't consider it a decision but a qualifier.

CHAPTER 5 – HOTEL ROOMS, HOUSES, AND GIGS

You Can't Make This Stuff Up...

After living and thriving on the road, I can make do anywhere I have to live for a week or two. Here are a few very intriguing places. However, please don't set your vacation plans for some of these gems.

In the early days before 1977, travel mainly consisted of a tri-state area. A great memory of an uncommon and noteworthy booking is one that happened in 1975. This was before the consistent road days, and it is still one of my most cherished gigs.

We were booked into The Women's State Reformatory in LaGrange, Kentucky. We had no idea what to expect. It was only about a three-hour drive for us at that time. We loaded up all the equipment and off we went. The reformatory was a foreboding sight. We pulled up to unload equipment, and several women greeted us to help move all the equipment. There was a very steep, long stairway up to the concert hall/theater performance area. We got all set up then the women showed us where the "green rooms" were so we could change for the performance. These were some of the most courteous, welcoming, and kind women, and they were sincere in wanting to help make sure everything went smoothly. The women helped me with hair and make-up, which was outstanding since one was a make-up artist before lock-up. The entire visit was just spectacular. We were told that they were so excited to have us because live concerts don't happen very often there. Having a female lead singer and performer was the icing on the cake for them, and we all felt like stars!

In the 70s Marcus and I loved to drive around our area on most weekends, which included Louisville and other towns just across the river, to see some of the bands and the venues. Louisville had some fantastic venues. We booked ourselves into some of the places to get better at our music and live performances. We made friends with some of the musicians and talked to them to get information about who was booking them. We went to lots of concerts to see Chicago many times, also Ike and Tina Turner, Elton John, Arlo Guthrie, John Denver, James Taylor, Linda Ronstadt, and any artist that came to Louisville during the late '60s, early to mid '70s. It was sensationally fun, and we learned a lot. We gained lots of information from watching, and I felt like I could begin to get my plan in motion.

We played in hundreds of places and cities, but I have a few thoroughly memorable ones to share.

Chase on the Lake

Chase on the Lake Resort in Walker, Minnesota, close to the Canadian border, was one of our favorite places to go. This was a destination summer resort on Leech Lake. It was full of history, the presence of spirits that I could feel, and wonderous beauty. The people who owned it at the time were very accommodating to the bands who rolled through. It was big, old, and beautiful and had a lot of different spaces inside. It was very historic looking, exactly like it did when The Chase Hotel was built in 1922. When we were there in the late 1970s and the early 1980s there were landline telephones and minimal electricity in the rooms (people didn't spend much time indoors), a top-notch five-star restaurant, waterskiing, and other sports on the big lake where people from all over the world would come. We loved being there and everything about it. Recently, it was updated following a major fire that roared through the restaurant, the lakeside end of the hotel, in 1997. I was crushed when I found out about this, and I remembered my vision of our time there. Chase On the Lake was a big favorite, and the people were always remarkably kind and respectful to us. It was the perfect place to go for a summer getaway.

When Marcus and I were there with our early band members, the owners, employees, and guests all invited us to waterski, explore the town, and take photos with them. I remember the big Bittersweet trees in front of the entrance. I loved them so much and took lots of pictures each time we were there. The acoustics in the club were perfect, and musicians from all over came to sit in every Monday night for a weekly packed jam session. I can still visualize all the happy people, the grounds, and the expansive lake. The town was fun and an excellent place for tourists like me to explore. We played at this resort numerous times, and it was always like a paid vacation.

Rochester

In Rochester, Minnesota, we played in a venue that resembled the inside of a long, narrow train car. The stage was built up high looking over the crowd. This place was busy and much larger than it looked from the outside.

When I think back, two things stand out in my mind about playing in Rochester. First, the guy in the standing crowd who thought it was OK to puff on his big fat cigar right at the front of the high stage and blow smoke upwards into our faces, my face in particular. I was trying noticeably hard to ignore this guy, but what I really wanted to do was to kick him in the head since my foot was exactly his head level. That was one of the rudest things that happened in all these years. Thoughtless. When you're singing, you need to breathe deeply, and that was next to impossible, inhaling cigar smoke with each breath.

We asked him to stop more than once. He took that as an invitation to make it happen more often. Not such a nice guy. Eventually, we pleaded with the club manager to ask him to move somewhere else. Of course, he moved to the far side of the stage. Did it help at all? Maybe, but noticing that he sat down close to the stage and kept inching closer was not surprising.

Rochester Circa 1979

The other memory from this same place, which is kind of a melancholy one to think about, is the story of a woman who was a regular there several nights a week. She was a nurse and would stop in after her shift to hear a set or two before heading home. This woman had the kindness and joy of life that many people should tap into. When she smiled, she glowed. Going out with her friends was a great release from her busy job as a nurse. She wasn't there one weekend, and we thought maybe she had gone out of town to visit her daughter.

The friend she always came with to our shows hadn't been there either. The friend came back the next week and let us know that she had passed away in her sleep the weekend before and her daughter found her. It was very sad for everyone who knew her. This woman was someone who attracted others to her through her joyful energy. I hope her family is at peace.

Sioux City

One of my most cherished memories is of playing at a very large club in Sioux City in about 1983-84 with an immense, high-level show stage and a colossal dance floor below. This was one of our very favorite venues. We loved seeing all our regular fans dancing nightly like Monday was Saturday night, and the other weekdays were building up the fun for jam-packed weekends. A young couple was dancing directly in front of me one night. They both wore glasses, which made it so perfect for working some rock and roll visual magic. I could see their heads bobbing up and down with big smiles to every song. Their arms were in the air, and they were sweating so much it was like the sprinkler system had turned on in the room. They couldn't keep their glasses from sliding off their faces, so they took their glasses off and set them on the edge of that very high stage right in front of my piano then continued dancing the night away. It just so happens that this was the time of Devo and fun, shiny mechanical-looking Devo glasses. In my stage gear, I had four pairs of Devo glasses that the band wore for certain songs. I saw the couple place their glasses on the stage and before they could notice, their daily wear glasses magically turned into green and purple Devo glasses. They didn't see me switch their glasses and were astonished to see that something magical had occurred. They joyfully and ecstatically grabbed the Devo glasses and put them on immediately. They wore them the rest of the night until the final song when they traded them for their everyday spectacles. They will never forget that night of illusion and wizardry, and neither will I. Music makes magic.

80s Devo glasses

The Haunted Wagon Wheel

I love hauntings and paranormal activity. We had a booking somewhere in Wyoming at a hall where there was a band house/apartment at the top of the club. It was seriously cool, not too big, but had three bedrooms, a kitchen, and only one bathroom. But we made it work. I always got first dibs on the bathroom, and no one seemed to care. I say this because the bathroom has a specific role in this story.

The first time we ever played there, we had heard previously from a couple of other bands that the place was haunted. Of course, we laughed it off but secretly hoped that was true. They told us about the things that had happened while they stayed there. So, we thought, let's just wait and see. During our first full day there, we rehearsed vocal harmonies in the afternoon up in the apartment, then later in the evening, we got dressed and headed down to play our sets. We finished the sets at 2 a.m. and headed up the stairs to the apartment.

What's the first thing you do when you get off work? Right, you want to watch a little TV, eat something, do a short workout, read a book, visit with friends, or do whatever. That's what it's like when you get done at 2 a.m. as well. We gathered in the kitchen and living room and thought someone was in the bathroom with the door open, but everyone in the band was in the same area, and there was no one else in the apartment. One of the guys got up to check, but no one was in there. The water was running in the sink. I don't mean just a drip; I mean a faucet on at full blast. This is one of the things the other band told us would happen. We just shut it off. It came on again just a few minutes later, so we shut it off once more and hoped that was it for the night. But we were eerily curious about the occurrences and having fun with it at the same time.

Next, we all heard footsteps on the roof. No, not squirrels and not birds, not raccoons. We were up at least twenty feet up or higher at the very top of the big old dark building. These were "humanlike" footsteps that started to run, then walk, then run. Now that was weird. Of course, our noses and ears were pressed against the walls and windows, but we couldn't see anything since it was on the roof and there was pitch-black darkness outside. When it stopped, we all went to our rooms to bed. I don't remember if any of the noises or water running happened again that night. Most of the band was sober, and we all loved the weirdness of it all.

That happened every night while we were there. After the first few days of living there, the water in the bathroom came on in the afternoons, too. We stayed there probably three times over the years, and the same things happened. Occasionally, a light would start flickering, or a strange chill and mist-like substance would emerge from one place in a particular room. Ever get that feeling that someone is watching you while you sleep?

Dickenson Band House

At most places we played, we were accommodated in hotel rooms. Other venues provided a band house, which was usually a medium to large-sized house in decent condition with three or four bedrooms. We liked that because there was always a kitchen and other amenities that we didn't usually have.

It was springtime with beautiful weather. We were in a four-bedroom, two-bathroom, well-kept band house in Dickenson, North Dakota. The club we played in was massive and just a short drive from the house. We got there on a Sunday in mid-April. After unloading and setting up equipment and sound checking at the club, which was close by, we immediately got out lawn chairs that were in the garage of the house and soaked up the 75 degrees and sun. We went inside when it was getting dark and had a nice, uneventful evening.

When we got up the next day and tried to open the front door, it was not opening, it was stuck, like something big and heavy was pushing against it. Checking out of the windows, we realized it had snowed at least three feet overnight, and drifts were up to the roof overhang of the house. Overnight the beautiful spring weather decided to turn tails. It's a good thing that we had put the lawn chairs away and parked one of the vehicles in the garage the evening before.

The snow and drifts were so high that we all had to force open the garage door from the inside and shovel our way out so we could get to the club that night. Because it was impassable by vehicle, we walked to the club because there was no way to drive through this. But what happened next was a sight to behold because all the people in the surrounding neighborhoods were doing the same thing, walking to the club to hear us with snowmobiles buzzing behind them. There were so many people walking with us, it was inspiring. We were all doing a high-knee march through the depths of that snow. A little snow won't stop Midwesterners. That image and its impact are still with me. I can see all the people making their way on foot in the big deep snow to have a great night of fun and music. It wasn't always that kind of weather in North Dakota, thank goodness. Sometimes, it was extremely hot and sunny; sometimes, it was a perfectly clear spring or summer day.

Urban Cowboy at The Red Stallion

One of our engagements was at the biggest venue in the area we were in. We played at this club many times. It held a few hundred people, had a big concert stage, a balcony all around the entire club, and drew a wild, brawling crowd. This was during 1981-83, and the music was extremely fun. It was a rowdy and loud place. There were drugs and lots of alcohol everywhere, which made it raucous and, at times, seriously unruly. Dancing, fun, and full-on pandemonium reigned as each night of the week passed without much incident, except for a few drunken arguments between couples and a brawl or two, until our last night there for this current gig.

At the end of the last set, Bruce had gone towards the green room, which was a large break room for the bands next to the stage. Rob followed him in that direction. As soon as Bruce went inside and before he could close the door, Rob, who was extremely high on whatever he was using, plowed through the door, broke it down, and tackled Bruce to the floor. Fortunately, Bruce was able to push him off, and a couple of guys, including the manager of the club who saw this, pulled Rob away. This was one of the few times this type of thing happened. Bruce and I had decided to finish the scheduled shows through the end of the next month, then planned to leave and put our own band together. Of course, after the next day, things had cooled down. But this kind of action transpired more than once after we announced we were going to leave.

Dickenson Band House Take Two

The next gig was a return to North Dakota where we had that beautiful big band house and April blizzard. Tempers were still simmering due to our decision to leave. At that band house, a rift between Richie, the drummer, and Bruce flared up. On our last night there, Richie was beyond bitter that we were leaving. He was so enraged that he began to taunt us. This was the last show that Bruce and I had to play before we planned to leave this band, and you will read more about that in the chapter on Dangers. What ensued that night was a bloody fight club scene between a few of the band members. I will guarantee that drugs and alcohol were the underlying factors in this absurd fight. When it was over there was blood spatter on the walls and some needless other things that happened to make it look like a crime scene. No weapons, just fists flying and bad drunken fighting moves, leaving Bruce with a broken nose and some black eyes for all involved.

Band House/Fight Club House in Dickinson, North Dakota

One Place of Many in Texarkana

In about 1986, when Holiday Road Band was at the height of popularity, we were sent to Texarkana, Texas. Spending all those years playing full-time had its challenges and weirdness, rewards, and accolades, but this place took the prize for strangeness.

We were usually at a place anywhere from one to seven weeks at a time, playing five and six nights a week every week. Bruce and I traveled with our four ferrets, our drummer traveled with his little dog and two birds, and our bass player had a sweet old cat named Roadie. We all kept our hotel rooms decent since we had to live there all that time and wanted to get invited back. We were not musicians who tore up rooms, although we traveled the same highways as they did. Every hotel or house had designated band rooms or a band house where we lived during our time booked there, and musicians were all treated the same way until you proved you were respectful of the place. I insisted that my guys were always respectful of the places we stayed and to other paying guests. We left our rooms in good shape and tried not to be noisy in the halls at two in the morning and later.

As usual, we had a food bill and beverage bill that every one of the band members paid their portion of at the end of each week as we got paid. This guy, however, the hotel/bar manager, who was, shall I say, a little bit (or a lot) alpha male, decided that on our last week there, while we played our final set of the night, he would lock us out of our rooms and not pay us until the restaurant/bar tabs were all paid. None of us could get our room keys to work. Yep, no access to our belongings or our pets. They allowed pets, so we knew it wasn't that. I spoke to this manager and asked why we couldn't access our rooms. We reminded him that we would gladly pay our food and drink bills after we were paid for our time and work (and yes, it is a lot of work).

This was not making much of an impression on this guy, so I decided to talk to the owner. After I called the owner of the hotel at about 1:30 a.m. on that night/morning, we got back into our rooms quickly, as the steam roller of a manager looked like he was going to blow a gasket. It boiled down to being a female and in charge, which he didn't like at all. The female staff mentioned to me how they had been treated since working there. It wasn't good. I told our management to cross that place off the list. During this run, one of the band members was ill with bronchitis at the time and still performing. We don't get to call in sick, but that guy noticed we had one less person singing. The hotel manager just gave me the deep-set evil stink eye for fixing the situation when he thought he could bully us, especially the chick in the band. As a woman band leader, there were more times than I wanted to count that it was hard-pressed for me to get the dignity and respect that most males would get in situations like this.

Next up, the worst of the bad. Teen Slasher Movie House

I don't remember where this band house was or what city we were in, but when the club owner led us out into the country, we were thinking, hey cool, a cabin in the woods, either that or he's going to murder our group of young people and hide the bodies.

Picture this…Big golden fields, lots of trees, close to the city and the club. It was quiet, green, and off the highway. Sounds pretty, peaceful, and unbelievable, right? Well, it certainly was all of those things…and more.

We drove up the long gravel driveway to an unfinished home that looked like someone had just stopped building for some reason or lost their building permit. There seemed to be no actual door, only a piece of plywood the size of a door. There were no locks or real windows, so we thought that maybe we should find hotel rooms somewhere closer to the club. The only good things were that it was free and that there was a full kitchen. Walking inside, we noticed a big, thick slab of foam on the living room floor that was not particularly clean. I mean, it was gross, stained, and perhaps a little bit chewed up from field mice or worse. Each of the two bedrooms and the living room had the same thing. If you're wondering about this, we asked about it. Those were the beds for the band. I didn't realize we were camping!

There were no doors to any of the rooms except the bathroom, and the bathroom was so small you had to go outside to change your mind. We turned on the water faucet, and what came out was brown. Pure rust! It was well water, not city water, and boy, did it smell like rotten eggs. Now, we were not prudes or super high class, but we, without question, expected to be treated with a little bit more consideration, especially for the length of time we would have to spend there. The owner was so proud that he had this 'last teen standing' horror movie house in the prairie. He told us he was building it all by himself and thought we'd like the quiet of the country. We asked about getting a lock on the front door. He immediately put a lock on the screen door. Well, that's helpful unless someone wants to actually break in. The plywood piece was still the unattached entry door. We had to slide it into place to go in and out. We covered the old mattress slabs with comforters that we bought at the closest discount department store.

Well, we made it work for the two weeks we were there. It wasn't pretty, but it ended up being fun if you like camping, which I do not, and getting dressed up every night in your tent. I don't know how, but we made the best of a strange situation and laughed about it while we were there because what else could we do?

During our load-up and move-out on the final Sunday, Jeff R.'s cat, Roadie was lost. The grounds were all high gold and green prairie grasses and solitude for as far as you could see. Roadie had gone outside into the field while we loaded our belongings into the vehicles so we could drive on to the next gig, not wanting to spend one more night there. He could have been anywhere.

We all decided that Bruce and I would start driving to the next gig and get checked in while Roger, our drummer, and his wife, Cindy, stayed back with Jeff R. to help find Roadie out in those tall, never-ending golden fields that had not been mowed for at least a year.

Luckily, Roadie was found. He had gone out exploring, then wandered back to the house after an hour or so. He heard his name being called and decided to take his time to come back. Everyone got to the next gig the night before we had to set up, and all was well. But we will never forget that one. I wonder if the guy who was building this house ever finished it and if he would seriously live there before completing the building. My guess is not in a million years.

Above: Roger at the scary Band House in the Woods

Road to the Teen Slasher Movie Band House in the Woods

Springville, Arkansas

Perhaps the hotel in Springville, Arkansas might have been another one in the top five worst hotels with a broken-down pool and broken-up pool furniture that appeared to have been tossed into the empty pool crater. We looked at each other and said that they must be remodeling. Oh wait, it gets better, or worse, I mean.

125

As Bruce and I entered our room, from the first step onto the carpet, a swarm of fleas flooded the entire room from said carpet, and there were some other questionable conditions in this room. I wonder who the last band here was. Maybe I just didn't want to know. We asked for another room before we took anything into that room. The management at this hotel told us they were so sorry and had no idea about the flea-ridden carpet. We got a key to a different room which was very clean and tidy. They did tell us that the property was up for sale by the current owners. I wish the new owners good luck. The club we played there was very nice and was run well, with a responsive crowd every night and people who were ready to be entertained. It was worth it all at that moment as the performances drew more and more people. We decided to tell our agent that we would love to go back as long as we had clean rooms every time. It turned out to be a positive venue. We were at the point where we could choose if we wanted to return to the venues we played or not. That status was well earned over the years.

North Dallas

Speaking of swarms of bugs, remember my story about the invasion of the grasshoppers when I was sixteen? At a two-week gig in a north Dallas suburb, we stayed at a beautiful convention-scale Holiday Inn. It was a sunny, summery September in Texas. Little did we know that it was cricket season. Yes, there really is a cricket season. Hot, dry weather brings them out. It was almost horrifying to see the building pillars, which were freshly painted white, turn solid black. The sidewalks, streets, cars, and hotel room doors were suffocated with noisy black crickets. There was a lot of creepy crunching going on under our feet and vehicle tires. Yes, this was real.

I know crickets are supposed to be good luck, and if you aren't too grossed out yet, there's more. Our hotel room didn't seem to have any chirping Texas-sized critters, or at least I thought. But a couple of nights into the first week, I opened a zippered makeup bag and guess what jumped out into my lap? If you said a stowaway cricket, you would be right. I promise that this time spent in Dallas wasn't near as wild as a hundred grasshoppers jumping and flying into my sixteen-year-old face and my lap out in that lawn chair. We eventually went back to the same venue in North Dallas many times, but not always in cricket season, thank goodness!

Bridges in Illinois

I would have to say that the very worst of the flying insects was in Illinois. Crossing a bridge over a river in July during mayfly season, which is in the middle of summer, it was slippery on that bridge just like we were traveling on a sheet of ice. It was nasty and disgusting, and our vehicles and tires were covered with smashed mayfly slime. Homes and businesses were covered with them, and sidewalks and streets were covered with them. Insert your favorite expletive here. They are a gruesome, obnoxious, unpleasant, sticky, scummy, large flying insect.

The houses and hotels we stayed at in a city or town were included in the contract. Most of the hotels gave the same rooms to the band members from every band passing through. Most of those rooms were very nice, clean, and comfortable. It was always unfortunate that certain bands decided to tear up their rooms before they left only to leave a bad impression on the next group of musicians coming in. I suppose they thought it made them look like rock stars. In my mind it was senseless and made them look disrespectful, maybe even deplorable.

Some of the things we heard about were smashing and grinding food into the carpets, like potato chips or spilling liquids, throwing, and breaking telephones, mirrors, flipping mattresses, and more that I won't bother to mention because anything you can think of happened in those rooms. This is the reason bands were always placed in the same rooms. In my logical head it just never made sense to destroy these places. These are rooms we lived in for a week or two or sometimes more. The agencies were responsible for making sure the bands who did this paid for damages and repairs. Believe me when I say these musicians wanted to have the reputation of big-time rock stars, and they ended up not being asked to return and broke from paying for damages and big bar tabs. It seemed a lot easier to me to just not do any purposeful damage.

The Plains, Huron

A venue we frequented in Huron, South Dakota was The Plains. The Plains was one of our favorite places to play. We loved it there. It was a large motel and entertainment center with a bowling alley, an 80s video game area with Tetris, Pacman, Donkey Kong, Space Invaders, Asteroids, and much more.

When we first pulled up to this club, we saw a giant twenty-foot concrete pheasant on top of the building. It was comical, and we weren't sure what to think. As we got closer, we could see arrows in the concrete bird. When we asked about it, the staff told us that hunters stayed there during hunting season, and they would get drunk and shoot arrows into the bird structure. To us this was hilarious, and hopefully not dangerous. It turns out it was not at all dangerous, except for a drunken hunter or two who fell down once in a while. It was just very funny and weird. The Plains was the place to go in this area, and people from all over the Midwest and beyond traveled there.

The Plains in Huron circa 1984

The Plains was an all-inclusive entertainment center that housed a large supper club that was beautifully set up with four-to-five-star worthy food. The large stage was at one end of this club. Volume was never an issue there since we started our sets at the usual 9 p.m. time and the area could easily seat over a hundred people. The tables were moved, so there was an enormous dance floor. The stage had a rising curtain and a spacious backstage with a green room. We took our video camera and made funny commercial spoofs behind the scenes. I still have some of those on poor-quality VHS tapes. They are still so much fun to watch. All the bands who traveled through signed their names on a big white wall of the green room where someone drew a big winding highway with buses and vans. We all signed that wall every time we were there.

We also made a couple of movie trailer-type videos that included the big pheasant, a warplane that was on display, and other interesting things around the lake. It was seriously lots of fun. Bruce and Roger developed their skits as they performed them. "Killer Pheasant" was our favorite. Cindy and I were cracking up with laughter until tears rolled from our eyes uncontrollably.

While in Huron we met a young guy named Brad, who played outstanding saxophone. We got to know him throughout the times we were booked at The Plains, and he asked us if he could sit in and play with us on some songs. The answer was of course, yes. Brad was a natural musician and was able to not only play the correct parts of songs but also played brilliant improvisation. Each time we returned to The Plains he sat in with us.

I researched to see if this venue was still alive. It has turned into a casino with much the same vibe, and the giant pheasant is still on top of the main building overlooking the city of Huron. I have no idea if they ever pulled out the arrows. In the back of my mind, I hope they didn't because it was just so comical and classic for the venue.

Gulf Shores Dream

The most perfect place we played and stayed was Gulf Shores, Alabama, just a quick drive from Pensacola. This was a real tourist town with anything and everything a tourist could want in a beach town. Aside from all that, the white powder sand, clear turquoise water, the numerous clubs with live music, and lots of perfect tourist shops, it always felt like a beautiful dream that we never wanted to wake from.

Bruce and I played various clubs in the Gulf Shores area and loved every one of them. This was Jimmy Buffet territory, and his

Margaritaville club was incredible. We went there to see it and hang out but didn't play there. The best part was seeing the beauty and feeling the love of this beach every single day. We played in Gulf Shores at least four times a year in different seasons and helped open up for bigger-name acts. Our venues and hotels all looked out over the ocean to seabirds, dolphins, seaplanes, helicopter rides, lots of buildings, and more people at certain times of the year than you can imagine. Everyone was happy in these surroundings.

The one downside was the oil slick problem from oil tanker spills. There were days, even weeks when we would walk on the beach and see big globs of black tar that would stick to our feet, shoes, carpets, anything and anywhere. The hotels had quite a time keeping up with the mess, but it never deterred us from returning. We felt that it just might have qualified as another paid vacation.

Landscapes

Traveling weekly and seeing so many different areas of the USA and Canada was like a three-dimensional atlas. There were no GPS devices then. We bought big Rand McNally atlases at gas stations and kept them handy. Navigating with the atlas was one of my favorite things while we drove. I would mark an X with a black marker for every city and town we played in. We had to get new ones about every few months or so since highways and byways were ever-changing. I went through the new atlases page by page to make my black X marks and add new ones. I took it on like it was part of my job. I loved those big old atlases and still do.

Before all the 'no smoking indoors' laws were in effect, every concert hall, bar, and venue had the same smell, or a better description would be stench. It was the odor of beer, smoke, liquor, cleaning fluid, sticky floors, walls, and periodically someone's thick, heavy perfume or cologne. And that was after the place was cleaned for the next night. The odors of cleaning fluids just blended in with the rest of the familiar essence. Our clothes, hair, skin, and equipment smelled the same since nicotine is sticky, and all the other odors stuck to the nicotine. It turns everything a dingy ugly yellow and brown.

It's interesting that our olfactory system gets used to things we smell every day. I'm not even sure when those laws began to take full effect, but it was a good thing for me, my equipment, and my sinuses to ban indoor smoking. Of course, the designated smoking sections in some restaurants or other places didn't clear the air very well at all. So, when the all-inclusive indoor smoking ban finally happened, we were so happy. Any place we walked into before that ban smelled literally the same. Big or small, that was the odor. After the no-smoking laws took effect, those places still smelled the same, and it took years of repainting and cleaning solutions to finally break apart that sticky nicotine mixed with the beer and liquor smells that had seeped deep into the carpets. Every time we were in one of our favorite places, we could undeniably notice that it was getting cleaner and breathing was easier.

The scenery we encountered on each journey was truly wonderful, and each area was different from the one before. Even the air in each place on the map felt and even smelled different. One place was soggy and saturated and smelled as if it had just rained, but there was none in sight, like Houston's thick, sticky wet humidity with air quality warnings not to exercise outdoors. Another would be dry and clean with clear skies like in Canada. During some of the colder times of the year, the air was thin, and it was hard to breathe, and the same place in the middle of summer was so hot and heavy that it was even harder to breathe. In the hills of Kentucky, Tennessee, and Virginia, we marveled at the giant green bears and other animal-like sculptures made from all the vegetation of leaves, ivy, and vines that covered the phone and electrical lines.

We had cameras, the old kind, that you had to get the film developed but the pictures always looked yellowish, sepia, or blue and utterly unclear. My Polaroid Swinger camera was my favorite in those incredibly early days to take photos, outdated by current standards, because the picture developed right after the camera spit out the square, framed in white photo. I still have those photos somewhere. Since I grew up in Southern Indiana, the big giant plant animals seemed always to be my favorite roadside view. It always felt like a fairytale.

I was captivated by the red dirt and clay in parts of Oklahoma, Texas, and Kansas. I would take photos of it because I felt like I had been there in another life. The flat land in these states went for miles, and if there was a thunderstorm, the lightning became nature's magic light show. If a tornado was coming, it would be visible for miles, even from other states. The black dirt in Iowa always looked soft and fertile. All the green and gold fields of corn and wheat were always glistening in the sunlight. The 24-carat gold giant hay bales rolled up on the green fields in the bright, clear sunshine, the horses and cows, goats, and sheep, I never wanted to miss seeing anything, no matter how mundane it might seem to someone else. And you could smell all of it, bad, good, or just outdoorsy.

Canada is breathtaking, magnificent, and clean as if it had fallen from the sky for us to behold and breathe in the crystal-clear air. The people are kind, and the scenery will imprint itself into your mind for life. On the other hand, shopping in Canada was definitely superior to shopping in most places other than big USA cities like Minneapolis, New York, Houston, and Dallas. I think you get the idea. If you have the opportunity to go to Canada, please go, take a deep breath of clean air, and thank me later.

Somewhere in Winnipeg, Canada Circa 1980

"It's those changes in latitudes, changes in attitudes

Nothing remains quite the same

With all of our running and all of our cunning

If we couldn't laugh we would all go insane"
~Jimmy Buffett

Next to the multi-vegetation and ivy-covered animals, my all-time favorite has always been the soft, powdery white sand and clear-as-glass turquoise water of the beaches in Gulf Shores, Alabama, and Pensacola, Florida. They pull you in and grab you tightly as if to keep you sheltered. To leave is to wake from a dream. Once you go there, you feel like it's where you always belonged. Just don't get into the water at night when the stingrays and sharks are feeding. But those Alabama blues and greens can take your breath away and the starry nights are incredible. One of the song lyrics I wrote while Bruce was driving as we entered this area is called Alabama Blues and Greens.

The Black Hills of South Dakota is another place that holds my heart. There are so many things to do and see in South Dakota. I never tired of everything it has to offer, from the Corn Palace to Mt. Rushmore, Black Hills National Forest. Black Hills is home to two historical monuments carved right into the towering granite peaks: Mt. Rushmore, and the Crazy Horse Memorial, which seemed to always be in some stage of build each time we were there. The Badlands feel like you're on another planet, with buffalo, wild mustangs, long-horned sheep and so much more to take your mind to other times and places. Deadwood was a place I knew I lived or visited in another life. The gravesites of Wild Bill Hickock and Calamity Jane and Seth Bullock are there in Mount Moriah Cemetery. Historically, my great-grandfather on my mom's side drove the Deadwood stage. Seeing it is like walking into the past. I seemed to know exactly where to go.

We always had a lot of fun at truck stops in every state that were big souvenir stores. There was always so much stuff there that we wanted to buy everything, and of course we did. We returned many times to all the same places on our travels, so most of the truck stops felt like home. It's like a mall of everything road-worthy.

Hiking on enchanted trails in Arkansas, where you can find every flora and fauna in the United States, is one of the most outstanding, perfect places. I called it The Enchanted Forest. It was a mystical place that Bruce and I hiked frequently when we were in the state. We always took a compass with us, but we usually got lost anyway.

On one of our hikes, we found a bookstore in the middle of the forest. It was like magic! We were on a part of the Trail of Tears, and this bookstore had anything and everything you could ever need or want to learn more about such as trees, other plants, vegetation, rocks, stones, and crystals in the state of Arkansas. They also had Earth Day merchandise and snack bars with dried fruit and nuts and bottles of water. We got more than a few paperback books about plants, edible plants, trees, and a cobalt blue Earth Day mug, which I still have. I always wanted to go back to that mystical forest bookstore but never got the chance. I don't know if we would even be able to find it again. It's a good thing we carried backpacks because we filled them up with our purchases. Those backpacks became much heavier, but the hiking was more fun and meaningful. Arkansas is the crystal capital of America. Trips to Mt. Ida were always on my travel list. Anywhere you drive while traveling in Arkansas, you can find crystal shops everywhere along the roadside. We made many stops at lots of those roadside rock and crystal shops. It's a state I have always loved to be in for traveling, hiking, and entertaining. After moving to Iowa, I ordered bags of crystals from one of my favorite wholesale crystal shops more than once.

Dayton, Ohio has the National Air Force Museum. That was extremely humbling and awesome to see. It was also home to some great friends we made with some other musicians, twin brothers, and their wives. One of the wives and I explored a noteworthy mystic book and crystal/rock store in the city. We walked in and saw that it was full of beautiful things to discover. A younger, small, eccentric man followed us from a distance as we wandered around the store. We turned and looked at him as if to ask why he was following us but seeing the look we had on our faces expressed that. He told me that I had the brightest green healing aura he had ever seen. I asked him if he worked there. He told us he did, but not as a salesperson, he gave readings. He asked if my friend and I would like a free reading since he was very captivated with us. We said yes, we would like that, hoping he wasn't trying to take us for all we had. He led us to a different area of the store, and we all sat down at a table. He asked if we wanted him to record his reading. I said yes, I would. After my reading, he wrapped a large green and red bloodstone with silver wire, put it on a leather strap, and gave it to me. I asked how much. It was free to me. I checked the prices of the stones on the way out, and a bloodstone similar to the size he gave me was around $40.

I still have the cassette recording and the wrapped bloodstone necklace from all those years ago. My friend was also interested in having a psychic reading. He gave hers for free as well. He told her that love surrounded her and asked if she had any rose quartz. She didn't, and he gave her a small heart-shaped rose quartz to carry with her always. This was spot on for her. She had been starting to feel that her husband was drifting away. She lit up with that rose quartz in her hands and later told me it helped her relationship. It was an interesting and enlightening time.

One of the sights we wanted to be sure to see in the vast spaces of Wyoming and Montana was Devil's Tower. It was 1978 and the movie Close Encounters of the Third Kind was released less than a year before our travels to the area, and we were excited to see it after being engrossed by the movie. Marcus and I saw the monument quickly from a distance. On our way there, it stood out for miles in the plains-like area of Wyoming. What a magnificent sight it was as we drove closer to it, it loomed larger and larger. We pulled up to Bear Lodge Butte and went inside. The history of this monument is etched in Native American storytelling and mythologies. It is breathtaking, and the stories are believable to those of us who love that culture and carry some of the genetics within us. Just walking into the lodge, I felt so much spiritual energy, energy of all kinds, and I wasn't sure exactly what it was from since it seemed to come from several directions. I just closed my eyes for a moment and could see some things that were happening all those years ago. The story of why Devil's Tower appears the way it does is based on myths about a giant bear and geological information about how it happened and why it looks the way it does. According to the traditional beliefs of the Kiowa and Lakota, a group of girls went out to play and were spotted by several giant bears, who began to chase them. In an effort to escape the bears, the girls climbed atop a rock, fell to their knees, and prayed to the Great Spirit to save them.

Devil's Tower Legend Photo Courtesy Travel Wyoming

As we walked the forty-five-minute hike around the base of the tower, we watched several people scaling the tower straight up. Looking up, I saw several climbing routes with different degrees of difficulty and different numbers of climbing tourists. The grooves in the rock looked deep and smooth. Walking around the base of the tower we encountered fallen rock, some vegetation, partly in the form of blue, white, pink, and yellow wildflowers, portions of the rock columns, or even entire columns of rock. Piles of broken columns, boulders, small rocks, and stones were at the base of the tower, indicating that it was once most likely much wider than it is today. The people who climb the tower are a big part of the reason this happens. My thoughts are that if people paid attention to what this monument means, they would realize that climbing it may, at some point, destroy it. But it is undeniably a phenomenal tourist attraction.

Am I sounding like a tourist guide? You should go there.

Devil's Tower from a distance taken with my Swinger Camera 1978

Entering cities like Dallas, Houston, Tulsa, Minneapolis, Nashville, or any big city with big city lights and skyscrapers never got old. Even being there several times before, we still felt the excitement and anticipation of each city. We didn't feel danger, and although the traffic was usually dreadful, we didn't feel swallowed up by the cities. We felt big and small all at the same time knowing that we would be part of each city and that there were people there just waiting for us and our music. When other people were at their offices, and other jobs, running errands, shopping, and going through their same lives and houses each day, we were driving into their city, getting ready to give them a nightlife so they could stop focusing on work, traffic, and just have fun. Seeing our names on the marques and sometimes a billboard, and having the opportunity to play in these metropolitan areas was worth every mile we drove, and all the traffic that, on any other day or having any other job, would prove to be a flat-out nuisance, as our friend Jon W. reminded us. Jon W. lived in McKinney, Texas, a suburb of Dallas, and had a two-hour commute to work in the city and back home every single day. When we asked why he would take a position where he had to fight the traffic for four hours every day, he simply said that he loved his job and that's just how it is there. I believe that is so true. When visiting my family in Houston or playing there, it always takes an average of two hours or more to get anywhere. No, we didn't have any cell phones to listen to podcasts or stream a music station. No Sirius FM, only old-fashioned AM/FM radio stations on the car radio and a cassette player if you had an updated vehicle. But I sure loved the radio and the extremely cool stations you could pick up, especially during nighttime driving. Stations carrying shows like Rick Dees, Dr. Demento, and fun FM stations could carry us into the next state before getting static. We just dialed in the next station that was playing the same radio show or something just as great.

Some of the great historical places we loved to explore and return to frequently were Gatlinburg, Murfreesboro, Chattanooga, Memphis, and especially Nashville, Tennessee; Colonial Williamsburg and Charlottesville, Virginia; Virginia Beach, and Charleston, South Carolina. Hiking the trails, if you are open and pay attention, you will be able to feel and experience some of the history that is so strong you can see, hear, and feel it especially if you close your eyes and listen. We went exploring there many times and always found something new. The hiking trails, touching the battleground sites that are still standing, the curious black bear cubs on the scenic drives, the waterfalls, and the stunning Great Smokey Mountains will make you want to return many times.

How The Holidays went for traveling troubadours…

Thanksgiving 1978 was unquestionably the strangest of my short twenty-four years and still holds that title today forty-five years later. Marcus and I were all alone in the hotel. The other band members had all gone to stay with friends or relatives for a day or two, the hotel restaurant was closed, no local restaurants, no grocery stores were open, just a gas station. We had to be back on stage on Saturday, so it was a nice little break.

I don't remember where this town was, but it was biting cold outside. Marcus and I walked a few blocks and got a couple of old-fashioned turkey TV dinners from the freezer section of the gas station store which was deserted except for the clerk and someone mopping the floor. The clerk was reading a book and had a television on in the background. We all said Happy Thanksgiving to each other. When the clerk looked up, we heard him say, hey, aren't you the band we saw last week? We said, yes, that's us, and this is our Thanksgiving dinner. Both of us and the two men working had a good laugh about that, and they said they were going to close the store up soon to go home to have their own Thanksgiving dinner, and that they would see us Saturday night.

We always traveled with a small microwave, so we heated up those frozen dinners, found a couple of old movies on television, and had a quiet, calm Thursday night. That situation showed us how to be thankful and how going inside ourselves helped us to find a bit of calm which didn't come easily amid the constant travel, band organization, and Marcus's sometimes volatile nature. It was a good thing for our relationship such as it was.

Another specific holiday while I was with Rob and his band taught me how everything is our teacher if we just pay attention. I think about all those holidays spent throughout the decades, who was there or not there for one reason or another, and the love and gratitude that expanded our hearts during that time.

However, this one Christmas stands out merrily. While living on the road, playing music in the 1970s through the early 1990s, most of my holidays were still spent with family, whether in Indiana, or Texas, then later in Iowa, or with the musicians who were my adopted family somewhere out there in the USA or Canada. The one that stands out is one that I spent all alone around 1981. Now, before you start feeling like "Oh no, not alone...on Christmas," you'll feel the way I did after hearing this part of the story.

That day ended up being possibly the most enjoyable, peaceful day I had ever experienced. I've always been a happy, positive person and very independent. But the thought of spending this Christmas Day alone was weird at first. So, I did the "I have no idea what to do" thing. Since it was sunny and strangely warm outside with melting snow on the ground, I decided to go out and explore the town I was in. Talk about a dead zone. Nothing was open, and not one person was anywhere, not a single soul. The stores and restaurants were all closed and even the doors to the churches were locked that afternoon. Since we had three days off, which was definitely not the usual, the other band members flew or drove home for the holiday.

Remember, this was before cell phones, email, and Google. So, I went back to the "band house" which was amazingly calm and comfortable. I loved this house from the first time we walked in. It was unlike any other band house or hotel we had stayed in. The best parts were the impressive bedroom photographic wall covers that looked like I was in a rainforest in Costa Rica, and the quiet patio with some comfy lawn chairs and beautiful forest-like woods surrounding the back of the property. I chose to sit back and hang out with the owner's Retriever puppy. The puppy, who had been my best buddy that week, came with me to just lay back and listen to nature. Even the dog, who was still a puppy, just sat there with me. As the afternoon got warmer, we listened to the trees, the breeze, and the pond water, and suddenly,

I felt the biggest wave of peace I had ever felt up to that point in my life surrounding me. This was the Universe wrapping its arms around me and slowing my life down for a day. I had never felt that kind of peace before. I was able to breathe slowly, deeply, and deliberately. When I think of that day, I still take a few deep relaxing breaths and can see all of it. The puppy, the forest, even the lawn chair.

This is the point of my memory, the moral of the story. We had many opportunities to do the same thing year after year and even before that. So, whenever I feel overwhelmed, that's the place and the moment I go to in my subconscious. I have always been completely comfortable on my own and that's how it will always be. If you are your own best company, you're never lonely, and I never was.

I am surrounded by loving, strong, heroic people, including my family and my friends who are also family. I give them the best part of me every single day because that's how I feel every day. It helps me to be able to help them. But we all need to be renewed now and then to clear our minds so we can continue with life.

Before I met Bruce, I spent most of the holidays with my family in Indiana and Texas when everyone moved to Houston and the surrounding area in 1979-80. It was always a time I looked forward to. The fun of shopping, decorating, seeing my mom and sister, my brother, and his family, and all the usual holiday traditions. When Bruce and I were together, we would go to his family if we were closer to Iowa, and to my family in Houston if we were closer to that area. Those were amazing times of laughter, surprises, hugs, and cooking. My mom just loved Bruce and the dogs loved him too.

In Iowa, I always looked forward to spending time with Bruce's brother, Mike, and Mike's wife, Betty, whom I dearly love. I spent a significant amount of time on the phone with my mom and sister in Texas. It was exciting, bright, colorful, and warm with lots of their relatives, food, and music. Bruce and I would sit at the family upright piano to play and sing Christmas Carols. The next-door neighbors would stop over every Christmas Eve bringing their brass instruments to serenade us with their well-rehearsed Christmas music. We would all talk to my mom and sister on the phone (still landline times). If we were out of town or out of state, we would pull out our video camera and VCR, we were always doing something non-stop.

These days it's just quieter and different. Spending that quality time on in-person visits and phone calls was the most important and special aspect of every holiday season.

CHAPTER 6 – FRIENDS, FANS, AND KNOWING THE DIFFERENCE

These Are the Good Old Days

We've had hundreds of fans but fewer real and close friends on our journeys. The difference is this: fans are followers of bands and their music and ask for autographs and photos. A groupie, so to speak, is someone, female, or male, who is a fan of a particular band, singer, or other famous person and follows them around to places they perform, or attempts to sleep with the target of their affection or call until the phone is answered, goes to their hotel room, knocks on the door, asks them to go out, or invites them to come over to their home. Mostly, they are harmless people who love the band's music and want to get closer and be more than friends with a band member or the entire band.

Another type of fan or follower is a person or group of people who linger until the end of every show and then persistently shadow one or more band members, hoping to capture their attention. While this can be seen as a form of flattery, it can also be disruptive, especially when we're trying to unwind after a performance or pack up our equipment. If not curbed, this behavior can escalate into a more serious situation.

Both instances can, and sometimes do, turn into a stalker situation. Before there was any type of social media there were stalkers. These were in-person stalkers. It feels extremely dangerous to have someone drive past your hotel several times a day or hang out in a hotel lobby waiting to see if you'll come down the elevator or lurk in the hallway just to get a glimpse of you in case you open your door. Of course, these can be male or female fans. You might not recognize a stalker fan until they show up every single night alone, sitting in the back of a dark corner of the room. Seeing that same person night after night without incident is one thing. Seeing that person during the day in all circumstances is strange.

This happened a couple of times. My instinct told me to go to the person, talk for a few minutes on a break, thank the person for coming out to the show, then go to another table to talk to someone else, then head back to the stage. It seemed to work, letting the person know you acknowledged him or her. It seems simple, but it's not always so simple and can be dangerous.

While living in hotels, there were days when the hotel room phone rang early in the morning, and you had no idea who it was, but they invited you to a Sunday cookout. That's a very nice gesture. However, Sunday is our only vocal rest day, a travel day, or both. And early morning never works for us since we get to bed between three and five in the morning. Then, if you answer, you ask, "Who is this again?" And it dawns on you that it's the person who had been with a group of people at the gig last night who kept asking you to sit with them on breaks. They didn't want to leave a message at the front desk because they worried we might not return the call. So, they kept calling every hour.

One problem for us was that we entertained groups of people every single day and night, so going to someone's cookout or dinner where there would be a group of people meant a rest day was not going to happen. When they invited us, and we went, they inevitably expected us to bring a guitar or use one of theirs to sing something, to tell a couple of jokes, or to talk about our life story. So, we didn't normally go to these events. I don't blame these folks since they didn't understand, and I never felt comfortable explaining it to them for fear of insulting them. This was a different situation than when friends we knew well invited us over.

What about the fans who called the hotel room at 9 a.m. to ask if you wanted to go somewhere or do something? Again, it's a great gesture, but getting done with work at 2 a.m., unwinding, and getting to bed after 3 or 4 a.m. doesn't make a 9 a.m. phone call pleasant. It was always like a bad alarm clock. I understand that most people do not work our other 9-5, so it's not relatable to them. So, if I decided to answer the phone, I was always kind and explained that they should leave their number with the front desk, and I would call them later that day, which I always did.

Usually, these were my female fans who wanted to get closer as friends, those who would call me early in the morning whenever we were in her town to ask if I wanted to go to the mall, to lunch, or the pet store and play with the animals and tarantulas (that positively happened). Now, how could I possibly turn that down? One time, I didn't turn it down. I went to a local pet store in the city we were in, with a woman I will call Amy, and it was fun. But I had no intention of spending the entire day with her and her favorite pet store tarantula. Unfortunately, this woman decided we were best friends and called me every morning at about nine-thirty for the week we were in her town. I was always happy to see her when we were in that town, and she always came to the show each night. But we didn't keep in touch otherwise. I can only imagine if there were cell phones back then. After the third day, I asked her not to call at that time of the morning but to feel free to call after one or two in the afternoon. She thought half the day would be gone already if she did that. Her day would be half gone, not mine.

Real Friends – Found and Lost

*"Just yesterday mornin' they let me know you were gone Suzanne,
the plans they made put an end to you*

*I walked out this morning and I wrote down this song I just can't
remember who to send it to*

*I've seen fire and I've seen rain I've seen sunny days that I thought
would never end I've seen lonely times when I could not find a
friend*

But I always thought that I'd see you again" ~James Taylor

Robert

Our first encounter with HIV was in 1984. We met a wonderful man named Robert who quickly became a close friend of the band. Robert was kind, and intensely handsome, with dark hair and a strong frame. He was always generous and quite hilarious. We spent a lot of time with him every time we were at the club we played in his city. We got to know him well as he got to know all of us. Robert was a brilliant singer and sang with us some nights. His choice was to sing Madonna tunes. The audiences loved him and the fact that he sang Crazy for You and Like a Virgin made them love him more. No one caused any problems for him or us. Just the opposite. Everyone loved him and cheered for more. My feelings from these memories are all-encompassing, warm, and happy.

The last time we saw Robert was during one of the many times we were in town, and he invited us for an early dinner. I know what I said about invitations to dinners and events with fans. However, Robert was more than a fan. He was a friend we trusted, and we always loved the time we spent with him. This was on a Saturday afternoon, and we were all looking forward to playing that night, including Robert. His apartment was in a large, old, luxurious home. He had the top floor. I still remember how open the space was and all the beautiful wood flooring. When you walked into the dining room, it was so airy and bright, and the lighting was all natural from the big windows and the overhead lighting. His dining room table seated at least ten people. It was an aged walnut table, and so were the beautiful chairs, which looked like a photo from a magazine.

To say Robert was an epic chef would be almost a disservice to him. He served a fabulous Italian dinner in courses. He had exquisite clear crystal glasses for water and wine. The dinner dishes were a gorgeous set of designer quality with small green leaves and tiny blue flowers with a gold rim around the outer perimeter of each plate, bowl, and cup. We were blown away by his hospitality and the loveliness of his home, and we all had a glorious time. The background music, the laughter, the food, the sharing of stories, and the great friendship made it one of the most outstanding pieces of the traveling puzzle. Heartfelt, warm teddy bear hugs were abundant when we left for the evening. Our gig in this comfortable, familiar city was over for now, and we were heading out to the next location that very next day.

Several months later, when it was time to return, we learned the news that Robert's body had been abducted and his beautiful, young life snatched away by AIDS. Roger, Cindy, and I still talk affectionately and joyfully about our time with Robert. And there are times when I know he is present, listening in with glee and still singing his favorite Madonna songs.

Mark Monarch

In the mid-80s, we met a group of close friends who became good friends. They came to hear us several nights a week and were always there all together as a group. We didn't see any of them for a week, which was odd. They came to hear us as a group of two couples and one single guy and never deviated from that. When we didn't see them, we weren't too concerned until the next Saturday night. The entire group was there, but one was missing, his name was Mark. They came up to the stage a few minutes before we started our sets to tell us that Mark had been killed in an auto accident the week before. It wasn't the best time to tell us this, but there never is a good time. Mark was a calm, kind guy who usually put his friends before himself. This was such a shock to everyone who knew him. We played on through the night, and the group stayed until the end. The next day was Sunday, and we were leaving for the next town. Something magical happened on that Sunday.

As we loaded our equipment and belongings and headed to gas up the big band truck, a Monarch butterfly flew onto the windshield and stuck there. When we stopped at the gas station the beautiful butterfly flew from the windshield to Bruce and sat on his shoulder as he kept moving around putting gas into the truck. We watched closely as the butterfly came to me and sat on my nose, then moved to my hand. It stayed with us as we got back into the truck to leave. Bruce said that it was Mark, and he named the butterfly Mark Monarch. I feel he was right on about this instinct. It was lovely, and when we went back to that city to play again, we told the group of his friends about it. They told us about a Monarch butterfly that had been hanging around them all week after we left. Magic? You decide.

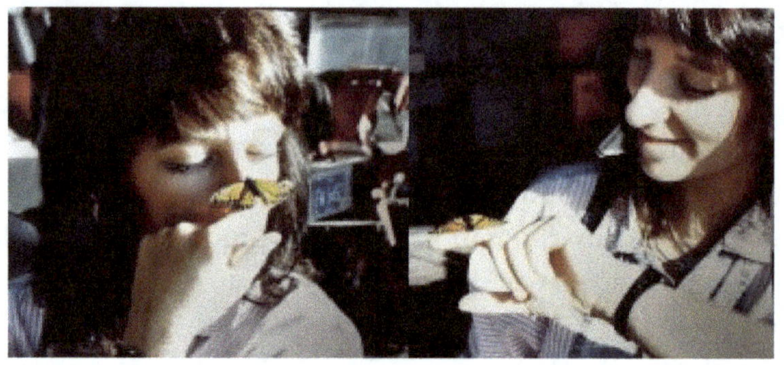

Mark Monarch 1985

Loni

In the earlier days, I met Loni. Loni is a genuine, true friend and has always been from the beginning. Loni came to hear us play whenever we were in her area. She lived in Minnesota and knew Paul and many other fans who came to dance and have a great time every night, and we were there a few times every year. Loni, her sister, and some friends would always be at the club during the week and especially never missed the weekends. She and I did lots of things together. There was a time when she and I decided that I should put my long hair into cornrows with colorful beads. It took hours for Loni and her sister to do all the work as I sat there while we talked and laughed. I was so proud of how cool my stage hair looked and felt. It was very Donna Summer and unexpectedly heavy with large, colorful wooden beads, and it swayed and danced to the music I was singing and playing. Only once did those beaded braids hit me in the teeth while swinging and swaying. That was a jolt! Whenever we were close enough for Loni to come and visit, I always called her to say, "Come and get me." And we'd go shopping, exploring and whatever we fancied. She told me that I gave the best directions to find our hotels. Those old atlases were great since that was essentially our only navigation source.

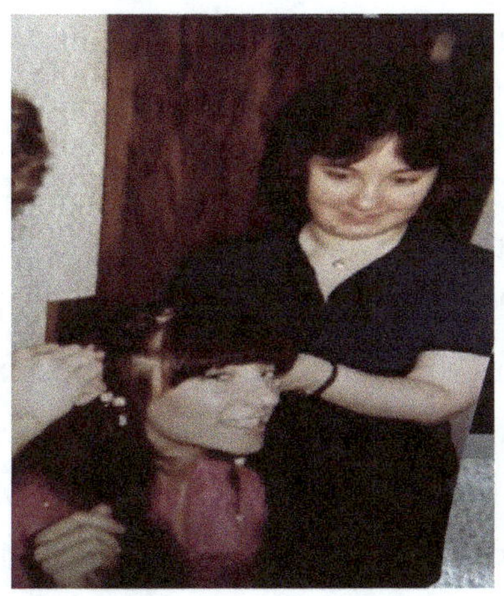

Loni and her sister doing my hair   **_Circa 1979_**

Loni and I have been friends throughout all these decades via cards, letters, and texts. We've been through the marriage of her sister, children born, deaths of parents, and a couple of moves for both of us. It's such a pleasure to know that we will always be in touch without even seeing each other again in person and be able to pick up right where we left off.

I did make some exceptionally close friends on the road, some of whom I keep in touch with after all these decades. We exchange Christmas and birthday cards, and many of them are Facebook friends. An especially close friend is one I made with a woman who was part of my satellite family from the day we met.

Kim, Kendall's, and Oklahoma City

Bruce and I played in Oklahoma many times. There was a great club attached to a nice hotel where we played two or three times each year. It was managed by my friend Kim and her then-husband. When we all met, we figured we would be friends for life, and that is exactly what happened and quickly.

We spent a lot of time with Kim, her family, and her family of staff from the world-renowned restaurant she owns (Kendall's) named after her first-born daughter. We both had an instant feeling that the Universe put us in each other's paths for a reason. We all became inseparable. We sang, danced, ate together, told stories, and spent time together whenever possible. Bruce and little Kendall, who was four years old then, became fast friends. Bruce was always very kind, caring, and amazing with children and they hung around him like he was a kid magnet. He did magic tricks for them, he paid attention to what they told him, he told them stories about their stuffed animals, and he always included them in the activities all the grown-ups were doing. He even wrote and recorded a funny song for Kendall on her ninth birthday.

Bruce and Kendall (circa 1987-88)

Kim, her husband at the time, and their young daughter, Kendall, made it feel like home to us whenever we were there. In 1991 we decided to do a residency in the club in their city, which was tremendous. No traveling for us for at least a couple of months.

This is when Bruce became extremely ill. Kim and her family never hesitated once to get help for us. Bruce, who was beginning to show hard signs of alcohol damage, had vomited a substantial amount of blood and needed to be hospitalized fast. The EMTs took him to the nearest hospital. It was decided that he needed to go to the bigger hospital in Oklahoma City. He had lost seven of the ten pints of blood we have in our bodies and had become comatose. They could not airlift him due to blood loss and the pressure from internal bleeding, so the ambulance sped off to the hospital that would take him several miles away. Kim drove me to the hospital as fast as she could, staying as close as possible to keep up with the speeding ambulance. We all got there, and Kim didn't leave my side. My mom got to Oklahoma from Texas as fast as she could. We all stayed in a hotel close to the hospital. To this day I don't know how I would have managed without Kim and my mom. It was all surreal. The doctors said if he didn't wake up in the next three days, he would pass.

You already know the story of Bruce's passing from the first chapter. Kim and I were always in touch during his ten-year illness after we moved to Iowa City, and even now, we remain close friends, and it still feels like family.

Today, Kim is remarried to a remarkable man and has a new extended family to shower her love on. This woman is part of me for life. Kim is gracious, generous, smart, fun-loving, and extremely kindhearted. She is compassionate and works harder than anyone I know. She is an incredible mother to her two daughters. Her younger daughter is a singer/songwriter and performs all over the area. Kim makes it a point to be at every one of her shows and is incredibly proud of her daughter, Kat. Kendall, her oldest, started out producing and editing movies and videos and now owns a top-rated hair salon. Kendall is also a gifted photographer.

Sara and Ed

After moving to Iowa City in the mid-90s, Bruce and I made friends with all the local musicians and played around the area at various venues. Iowa City/Cedar Rapids is a live entertainment metropolis with lots of music, Broadway show-type venues, and an all-around area where people travel to see all kinds of tremendous entertainment and sports.

I made a wonderful friendship with a couple named Sara and Ed who were musicians. We were drawn to each other from the day we met like we'd known each other in a previous life. They were a striking couple with big personalities and even bigger hearts, and we became friends instantly.

As we got to know each other, I learned that Ed, who was hemophiliac, and Sara were both HIV positive. They disclosed to me that Ed was HIV positive from a blood transfusion he received and Sara from her ex-husband, who was a drug user and who still lived in Texas. The two friends became a couple from their interactions in hospitals and clinics. They moved in together. This was a loving, caring match between two inspiring souls who knew their time on this planet was limited. Sara and Ed watched out for each other, making sure that each other was safe in their home and living conditions, and made it to every one of their medical appointments. They both had adult children living in other states. It was strained and hard for them to communicate with their adult children, even though they tried and did their best, given the situation and the times.

Sara loved fun, beautiful barrettes and hair clips and would sometimes gift them to me for my hair whenever we saw each other. They would always come to clinic and hospital appointments together, holding hands like two teenagers. I loved it.

One morning, a call came in from Sara, and she was crying and almost screaming. She had come home, and Ed was lying on the floor unresponsive. She was devastated and completely lost. Ed had fallen and bled to death internally. Sara didn't know what to do, how to live, or even how to breathe. The years they spent together knowing this day would come but hoping against hope that it wouldn't be anytime soon came without warning.

After the mortifying and overwhelming plight of Ed's sudden passing, Sara's health quickly took a nosedive. I had hoped to keep in close touch with her during this time, but time wasn't on our side.

It was an ordinary day in April when I got a phone call from someone I didn't know. The woman on the other end of the phone told me Sara was asking for me and that I should come immediately. I said yes, I would be there. She gave me an address, and I drove as fast as possible to get there. When I entered the home, I saw several people I didn't know, and one of the women led me to a bedroom full of sunlight and flowers in vases.

Sara was lying in her large, soft bed, gently covered up to her chin. Her arms lay outside the covers, smoothed out so that no wrinkles showed in her beautiful, calming, soft bed cover with tiny pink and purple wildflowers. She looked emaciated but very beautiful. I saw light surrounding her and her skin was luminous. I sat on the edge of her bed, and she tried to reach out and take my hand, so I took hers. I told her that I was there. Sara had always talked to me about going back to Texas, where my family lived for many years, as well as hers. I told her we'd go together soon and that I loved her. A tear streamed from her clear blue eyes and glistened down her angel-like luminescent cheek. I grabbed her hand more firmly with both of my hands and waited. The woman who brought me into the room told me she didn't want to go until she saw me and that she was waiting. Then, it was my turn for tears of love and a life well-lived. She has visited me more than once since her passing, and I always know when she's around me because I can feel, hear, and see her. And I still have all the hair ornaments, barrettes, and clips she gave me. There was only one other time that I saw this luminous, angelic glow and it was just a short time before my mom passed away about fourteen years after Sara's passing.

Sara and Ed knew about Bruce's illness and that he was in the hospital just as much as they were. It was April of 1994 when Sara passed. I had only been in Iowa for a handful of months, but it felt like I had been there for years. Bruce passed away seven years later in much the same way and at the same age as Sara.

There is no end to all the friends and fans we have made over the years. We looked forward to seeing every single person anytime we were in town. I've kept hundreds of pictures that I can look through and try to name everyone in the photographs. It's impossible to do that, but I will never forget the feeling I always got and still get from those fans, especially those close friendships.

Kim and Kendall Circa 1997 Oklahoma

Bruce and Jon W in Dallas Circa 1986

With my good friend, Darlene Circa 1980 North Dakota

CHAPTER 7: THE STARS

Bright and Not So Much...

I'll begin this chapter in Fort Wayne, Indiana. We were at a major club in a beautiful hotel. Many times, any concert band performing in the area would stay at the same hotel as we were staying in especially since we did lots of college town gigs.

These were notable times in the music scene. It was 1984, and Madonna was beginning to emerge as an iconic star. There was Michael Jackson, Bruce Springsteen, Steve Perry, Cyndi Lauper, Stevie Nicks, WHAM, Phil Collins, REM, Patty Smyth and Scandal, Pat Benatar, Bon Jovi, Bryan Adams, Lionel Richie, The Cars…there were so many incredible sounds and so much star power talent at that time that are still set in the hearts of all who were alive and kicking during the 80s. The music of the time was truly unforgettable, and some of the stars who made it onto the charts from the 1960s were still charting in the 80s and even now are hitting the countdowns, like the Rolling Stones and Paul McCartney. It was a feeling of being able to rock the road with the freedom of bringing the best music to people wherever they are. It was such a massive, colossal feeling, and we were right smack in the middle of it all.

Van Halen was out on an extensive tour in the summer of 1984, and that night, they were staying at the same hotel for their concerts that weekend as we stayed in for the next two weeks in Ft. Wayne, Indiana. Some of their crew were heading over to the club where we were playing to get drinks and to see who the band was. It happened that David Lee Roth was coming with them but was asked to leave for being belligerent from what we were told. He was very drunk, very loud, very pushy, high, or both, and was not allowed to wander around the building. We heard some funny and great stories about him that week. The impression he left at the hotel in 1984 wasn't too favorable, but he was undeniably an outstanding entertainer and drew packed houses in the 80s. We didn't get to see too many concerts since we played five and six nights a week, but seeing Van Halen live in the early 1980s in Minneapolis was a trip! I only saw two concerts during that time. Linda Ronstadt was the other one I had the pleasure of seeing live in 1980 in St. Paul. She has always been my idol and is unmatched. I miss her and send her big love.

Earlier, in 1979, in Brainerd, Minnesota, during our Northern States tour, we played at a club attached to a large hotel/convention center in Brainerd, Minnesota. We had previously played there many times, but this time was unique. It was during the races at Brainerd International Raceway and Resort. The staff told us that Paul Newman came to Brainerd every year for the races and that he always stayed at the same hotel. Well, that's cool, but I didn't expect to see him. We went downstairs to the club one afternoon to get in some rehearsal time. I walked past the restaurant adjacent to the nightclub and glanced into the dining area completely out of habit since the two rooms were attached. I saw him sitting in the restaurant alone at a table by a large window. It was a truly celestial thing to see because all I saw at that moment was a bright beam of light over him from the sun, or was it from his natural glow in some astral plane and those piercing blue eyes? Talk about star power. Nothing was said, but he looked straight at me, and we exchanged smiles. I felt like I should move away quickly, which I did. The hotel and restaurant staff assured me he was a friendly and genuine person. I still have that vision in my head when I think about those times or see a Paul Newman movie.

Traveling in the mid-late 80s, we played on a rotation in Cape Girardeau, Missouri, a college town. Guns and Roses were a big act on the scene during this time, and we were at the same hotel.

Slash came down to the bar as we were on the stage for our sound check. He was already wasted. After slurring his order to the bartender, he dropped his head onto the bar. The crew that was with him shook their heads to say no to the bartender, then they managed to lift him to his feet and carry him out of the bar while his arms were spread out, and he appeared to be flying like an airplane, angling side to side. He was making airplane noises as he dipped side to side. It wasn't funny, it was sad. He is so talented. These days, he is better than ever and has cleaned up. He left Guns and Roses for a time and worked with Myles Kennedy before returning to Guns and Roses in 2016. A change was a good thing for this guitar wizard. I will say to anyone who bashes him or any star in this situation that the stage, the constant touring life, and how you feel from one day to the next mentally and physically can take a toll on every aspect of your life. Turning it around is how he saved his own life.

On the night of their concert at the college event center in that city, we were getting ready to start our show but noticed a commotion in the hotel lobby. Guns and Roses' drummer was in the lobby wearing only sweatpants with skulls on the legs of the pants. A line of young teenagers followed him like the Pied Piper. I watched as they followed him no matter what direction he was heading. We thought it was funny, and he appeared to be having fun talking to them as he led them through the lobby taking unexpected twists and turns.

After we had both finished our respective shows, all those teenagers followed them back to the hotel. Bruce and I had our hotel room door open just as we were getting back. Our phone rang. I answered it, and a young girl on the other end said, "He's in your room; I know he's in there." I asked her who she was talking about. She replied, "The drummer, the drummer, I know he's in there." I said to her, "No, he is not here." I thought this was funny, but clearly, I did not want them coming into our room, so I closed our door, and the phone rang again. Same kids, same words. It happened a couple more times, then I guess they believed me. But it was very amusing.

In 1984 Holiday Road Band was kicking some butt on tour and played lots of college towns such as Cape Girardeau and Ames, Iowa. I didn't live in Iowa then, but a few cities in Iowa were on our circuit regularly. This place was called Barnabee's and was packed out every night of the week, Monday through Saturday with a line to get in every time we were playing there, which was four or five times a year.

We stayed at the hotel on the grounds. Behind the property was a big, mowed field, and the band members would play football games between themselves while Cindy, our drummer's wife, and I watched. Since we stayed in many of the same hotels as big-name concert acts passing through the same cities and towns, we found ourselves opening for a few, and more than once, a star would sit in to join us.

HRB and friends Football behind the hotel 1984

One afternoon in the Fall, we saw two buses parked next to the field. Two big blue tour buses painted with 70s pop art and the name Blunder Bus pulled in and parked. It was Arlo Guthrie, his band, and his family. This was exciting for Bruce and me because we had always been fans of Arlo. In 1970, I went to one of his concerts. It was double the excitement at this concert since Linda Ronstadt was his opening act. They were both very young, and she was touring with Arlo. She performed barefoot and did the songs that started her career like High Muddy Water and Different Drum. Then Arlo came out, and the audience erupted in cheers. He did all the favorites and, of course, Alice's Restaurant. It was an event I would never forget from two of my all-time favorites, and I still see myself sitting in those rows right in front of the stage.

Arlo's Blunder Buses Circa 1984

We played for two weeks at Barnabee's, our usual place, on the grounds of the hotel we were all staying in. We had gotten to know Arlo and his family throughout the entire first week, and on Saturday night, after his concert, Arlo and his band came in to listen to us. His wife, kids, and band were all with him, and we all became easy friends that week. His band was performing at The Machine Shed, an Iowa State University area venue.

During our performance on Saturday, after Arlo and his band got back from their show, they sat in with us and played a couple of his most famous tunes. Then his band kicked into Start Me Up (Rolling Stones). His son, who was about fourteen then, sat in on drums. His entire band took over our instruments, and then something so normal for me was questionable for Arlo as he got up to play Key to the Highway and City of New Orleans on my piano. In his incredibly cool Arlo voice, he stated,

166

"This is weird…"

I can still hear him say it now, just as if he was standing right in front of me. My piano then was the newest and best gear, an 88-key Yamaha electric grand set up with adjustable legs on concrete blocks so I could stand up to play. The entire week was splendid, ending with an extremely fun Saturday night. Spending the week with the Guthrie family and band made it warm, refreshing, and inspirational. To this day, I am friends with Arlo and have followed his kids and grandkids, who are all making music.

Arlo on my keyboards at Barnabee's Circa 1984

Arlo and me backstage at Barnabee's 1984

I have no recollection of where we were when we had some fun in a hotel lobby playing a grand piano with a band member from Kool and the Gang. Bruce and I wandered into the lobby before our show, and we could hear someone playing the grand piano in the lobby. We had to see who this fantastic player was. Kool and the Gang had a concert and stayed at the same hotel. This was about 1986 when they were high on the charts. The piano player knew who we were from our posters in the lobby and asked us to sit down and play along. We loved improvising with other musicians. Bruce sat down, and the two of them took off like seabirds in flight. It drew a small crowd and was a pleasure for us. We didn't see each other again, but he did leave us a note when they left the hotel saying good luck and safe travels, my friends.

On another occasion in Ames, Iowa, when Bruce, Roger, Cindy, and I were going for dinner, The Highwaymen, Waylon, Willie, and the boys were there to perform at Hilton Coliseum. Again, staying at the same hotel, suddenly we noticed that we were all walking across the street to the same restaurant. They all looked at us as we all waved and nodded to each other. We didn't get the chance to spend any time with them, but just crossing the street with the three of them, Waylon, Willie, and Kris (Kristofferson), was enough to make anyone fangirl on these greats.

If anyone were to forget that the stars are just like anyone else, we can tell you that we had so many encounters to remind us that we are all people. We all want to bring the joy of music to anyone and everyone we can touch. We exchanged autographs and stories with some of the greats, hugged, shook hands, talked of our lives, and had an extraordinary time over the years.

CHAPTER 8 – DANGEROUS

Oh Baby, Baby it's a Wild World

Tornadoes, downpours, hurricanes, and other weather disasters don't scare me because we can't do anything about them except take safety precautions and deal with whatever happens. We know they aren't coming for us specifically, and we know they haven't been stalking or watching us.

I have had to deal with these things and more in my life and have pretty much handled everything in a determined, take-charge manner, not being afraid of anything happening to me. The first time I was seriously frightened was in the spring of 1977 in Gainesville, Florida. This was our first full year of traveling full-time, year-round.

I was twenty-two, and we were playing at a spacious club at an exquisite Holiday Inn in Gainesville, Florida where we also stayed. This was the time when hotels had the best nightclubs. This occurred during our first few months out on the road. There was a mall across the highway from the hotel and, of course, I had to go check it out. We'd been in Gainesville before at the Brown Derby, so I knew the layout of that city pretty well.

I drove the band van up the road and across the highway to get to the mall parking lot. I parked, went in, and was oblivious to anything except the stores I wanted to look through. On the way out of the mall, I had no bags since I had just been window shopping that day. I was walking back to the van and noticed that a beat-up Robin's egg blue pickup truck stopped to let me cross over to get into the van. It was moving very slowly, almost waiting for me to back out of my parking space. I looked at the driver for a minute. He looked familiar, but not like anyone I knew, just someone I had seen more than once. Then I got in the band van, backed out, and drove to the end of the lane to turn. Looking in my rearview mirror, I saw that same blue pickup truck behind me. I turned left to leave the mall, not thinking too much about it.

The pickup turned, too. So, I got a little suspicious and turned down another row instead of exiting, and so did the pickup. I did that again a couple more times, and so did the truck. By this time, I started to get uneasy and was beginning to be very concerned. I sped up a little and turned onto the lane that would lead me out of the mall, and again, so did the truck, and he sped up, too.

Thinking quickly, I turned in the opposite direction of the hotel and got into a bunch of busy traffic hoping he would not be there when I looked back. He was about three cars behind, and I could see that he was quickly checking all his mirrors to see who was around and if there were any openings to get behind me. I did some excellent driving maneuvers, if I do say so myself, and got out of his line of sight. Then I waited before heading back to the hotel just turning back and forth on the city streets. I was fine but shaken and angry that someone would do something like that. Unfortunately, it happens more than we realize.

I know that I was not the only one this happened to in that area in 1977, but I got away. He had no idea who I was or that I was staying at the huge Holiday Inn across from the mall and I didn't see anyone stalking or following me after that. But I never went to the mall alone again. I hear it is being demolished now to build updated new shopping centers.

No matter how much you know about self-defense, when the actual situation occurs, you'll freeze, but use your head, you'll have a chance. I had not been through anything else like this exactly. We did not have cell phones to call 911 then.

Recently, while researching this book, I did an online investigation of crimes involving women in 1977 up to and including the early 2000s. The 70s were an era of serial rapists and serial killers for which there was no technology, DNA, or social media to help. I have been a true crime enthusiast since that day following the progression of technology. Many of these cold cases are being solved all these decades later, thanks to advances in technology.

Remember Rob from North Dakota? He was always working on his health by using powdered supplements, running daily in any type of weather, and appeared to have an unhealthy obsession with his thin permed hair and drugs. He was a father of two teenagers, and unfortunately, he was a drug user, a drinker, and a narcissist. He treated me as if no one else could ever touch me or even talk to me without his permission. Of course, I did whatever I wanted, which led to more than one confrontation. After an all-night after-party that I had gone to for about fifteen minutes to make an appearance, he came banging on my hotel room door. He was not a considerably big guy but spread himself out like some kind of bear in the wild so that he could force himself on me, which he did. Memories of my senior prom night came rolling back.

Interestingly, his girlfriend/fiancé, Joan (not her real name), was in the next room waiting for him to return from the party. My room phone kept ringing. Finally, I was able to free myself enough to answer it, with one arm out to try and stop him from pushing me back down on the bed. I told her to come and get him. That was the end of it for a short time. As it turns out he was engaged to her and would soon be getting married. Joan, of course, knew he was doing whatever he could with whomever he wanted. He had no problem getting other women because, in his mind, he was the most desirable human on the planet and many women loved his Tom Jones style. Joan was of the mind that he was going to marry her and stop all that nonsense. Right. She tried her best several times to help keep me out of his aim. Getting high on drugs was his thing, and it would turn him into that grizzly bear with unstoppable strength and speed. He thought it made him powerful enough to do things he couldn't or wouldn't normally do. He wanted me, and nothing was going to get in his way. And, yes, this treatment continued throughout the time I was with his group. Joan had the drugs with her so he would have a reason to come to her, and if she used the drugs, it was because he was using them, and she paid for them hoping that this would give them a bond of some kind. She probably thought that was the way to his heart. I don't believe he ever appreciated her for who she was.

Rob also had another bad habit. He shoplifted for the thrill of it, in whatever town we were in. He got caught once in Canada, and the shop owner called the police, who took him to the police station. There he begged them to allow him to pay a fine and return what he stole because we had a show that night. Since they knew who he was and who the band was, they let him go with a fine to pay. What a reputation to have. I had to get away from this.

After Bruce and I had played with this band for a couple of years, and after the big knockdown, drag-out fight club that happened with the drummer in the band house, as I explained in an earlier chapter, we decided to move on and form our own band. We were not ready to stop performing and traveling and had met so many artists and other road musicians who became our friends that it felt right to continue with healthier band members and play more of the music we wanted to perform. In Rob's group, we performed crossover country and pop. This is what the management wanted, and we enjoyed most of it. We even brought some of that music to the newly formed group. The current gig was over after one more week, which meant we could get out of the situation quickly, or so we thought.

On the day after the final show with Rob's band, we were getting our equipment and belongings which were packed into Rob's big red box truck we pulled up to his place and started to unpack from his truck, which he had unlocked for us that morning, and get it all packed into Bruce's vehicle. This was the same week as the big band house brawl. We emptied our band equipment from one vehicle to another then Bruce went back to the band house to get the rest of our clothes and packed cases as I did a second check to be sure we had the rest of our equipment out of Rob's truck. Like a crash of lightning, Rob bolted out of the door to Joan's house, where we were parked, and grabbed me so hard I felt like a sumo wrestler charged at me in the ring. At first, he slammed my right hand up against the wall of the box truck and, as I found out later, broke the ring finger of my right hand. I didn't even notice at that moment. I'm still unable to bend that finger at the first knuckle. We tumbled out of the van onto the grass, and he began to rage and proceeded to hit me in the face and head. It was so fast, like a tornado of whirling arms, that I fell back onto the lawn. He grabbed me up, my feet not hitting the ground, and forced me into the house, heaved me onto some furniture, and kept hitting and slapping. Joan, his soon-to-be wife heard all the commotion and ran to me, yelling for him to stop before he killed me or put me in the hospital as she grabbed at him. My adrenaline rose, and I was, indeed, not hurt much and was kicking and trying to elbow him, but he was strung out on whatever he had taken that day, and that made it impossible. I didn't feel much of anything physically, just the loud, blaring thought of getting away from him. By this time, Bruce, with his poor broken nose from the previous night, was back and was shocked but not surprised at Rob's actions. We'd seen him be completely out of his mind more than once.

Joan was able to calm him down and get him away from us. He had no idea what he was doing, but he kept saying to us that we couldn't leave, that I couldn't do this to him, why was I doing this to him? I don't know what happened to him after that and didn't mind if I never heard from him again. The last thing I was told by a mutual friend is that he was in a care facility with severe dementia, now in his mid-late 70s. Well, that figures. Did Joan ever marry him? And if she did, why? That's a mystery that will never be solved, but I hope she was brave enough to get out of that mess.

After getting checked at that same emergency facility we had been to the night before, for Bruce, I was fine, my equipment was fine, and we left to head out to Iowa. The only missing things were my little diamond earrings that I had purchased for myself in Canada a year or so back. During the scuffle, they had come out of my ears. I truly loved those earrings, but that's a small price to pay to leave that lunacy.

Moving on to the southern states:

Much later, while playing in another Southern Indiana city, we were at another large-scale Holiday Inn. We always put a Do Not Disturb sign on the door when leaving the room. We didn't want housekeeping service, and we were always allowed to get supplies and clean bedding when we needed it and to use the hotel laundry for ourselves. The housekeeping staff always asked if we wanted the room cleaned, so, of course, we did occasionally. The Do Not Disturb sign was overlooked or ignored a few times, and the housekeeping staff came in while we were gone during the day. On this unusual day, the weather was beautiful and sunny, and the pool was calling.

I decided to grab a lawn chair by the pool before it got crowded. This was a day of weird things happening. I got outside, plopped onto the lawn chair with a magazine, and loved the fact that I was the only one there. Later, two other women came out and sat on the opposite side of the pool. Then things got extremely strange.

A young guy, I would say in his mid-thirties, came out to the pool deck with a towel around his waist and chose a lawn chair a couple of chairs away from me. Then he proceeded to remove his towel only to expose himself in his tidy whitey briefs, yes, his underwear, his briefs. I looked at the other women; they looked at me. We were all trying to figure that out and making faces to say, what is that? But through our shock, WTH moment, and giggles, we all went inside, and that guy ruined our day in the sun. We informed the front desk about the guy, and he was removed from the hotel. He wasn't even a guest, just a guy from town or passing through who might have eventually proved to be dangerous. I never saw him again during our stay, but I did see the other two women, and we laughed about it nervously and vowed to watch out for each other while we were there. Why do women always have to watch their backs and look over their shoulder to be safe?

The next part of this strange day was not funny. When I returned to the hotel room, I saw that housekeeping had been in our room. Something was odd. We had the Do Not Disturb sign still hanging on the door. Bruce had returned to the hotel by this time and thought something was off, too. I asked him to help me check around. The bathroom towels were all gone and not replaced, and the cleaning bucket was tipped over, still in the bathroom. Our sweet ferret, Jackson, came peeking out from behind the door, and I assumed he had come out and scared the housekeeper so she ran out. My brand-new purple compact double cassette deck boombox was missing along with $100 I had saved out of our pay the week before. Bruce and I went to the manager and told him about it. As we walked through the hallways, I saw my small purple boombox on a housekeeping supply cart that was stopped in front of a room that was supposedly being cleaned. I grabbed it off the cart and looked for the money. I assumed that money made it into someone's pocket never to be seen by me again.

We went to the manager and told him we had found the boombox but not the money. We did not want to question the staff since it wasn't our place to do that. We continued to place the Do Not Disturb signs on every door of every room. I still do that when staying at a hotel. It works 99.9 percent of the time. It's that one percent that we have to be aware of.

Danger can be anywhere you travel. While staying with my mom for a week in Houston, Bruce and I went to a mall to look at new computers. This was about 1986, and Tandy computers were selling well from Radio Shack stores. We took our big white box truck, the band van we had traveled in with Roger and Cindy for several years, still loaded up with equipment, instruments, light racks, clothing, and everything we needed to get to the next gig. We found a knowledgeable salesman and bought the computer. He and one other guy helped wheel it out for us, and without thinking about it, we opened the big garage-type door on the back of the truck to load it. All our equipment, clothing, stage lights, and luggage were visible to those guys. Not to mention that he had my mom and sister's home address on the sales slip. We were usually very trusting of people until they screwed us over.

When we got home, we brought the new computer inside to set it up and learn how it worked. We had closed the big sliding door on the back of the box truck and padlocked it as usual.

Around 5 a.m. that next morning, my mom and sister's Rottweiler began barking. Have you ever heard a Rottweiler's bark? It will put fear in the hearts of villains. Looking out of the front window we couldn't see anything. We got up later and went outside to get something out of the truck. The padlock had been cut, and as we opened the door, we saw that Bruce's guitars, one of my keyboards, my clothing, and various other things were gone. One of the light racks was unscrewed from the side wall of the truck. The lights were there, just hanging from the wall inside the truck.

We went to the Houston police, and they took our information. Nothing ever came from it. We were leaving within the next two days. Our anger and frustration would have to wait.

We went to some of our favorite Houston music stores, including the famous Texas Music Emporium, to buy new equipment. My sister helped a lot. I found a keyboard, and Bruce found a new Fender Strat. He was a Stratocaster player, and once you have your favorites and play them every day and night, you need to start again with a new one because it will have a different feel—a little foreign. The same goes for keyboards. You need to learn how to set up and use new synthesizers, as well.

Clothing was easier. My mom took me to a couple of stores, and I found a few new things that updated my wardrobe for the stage. From then on, anytime we were at my mom's house, we backed the truck right up to the garage door so no one could squeeze in. In case you're wondering, the computer was fantastic and lasted until the next best thing came out.

In 2003, Marcus wrote me an apology email letter after twenty-three years of my leaving to get control of the direction I wanted to go and work with a different group of musicians in a different area of travel and away from Marcus's control. In this email, he apologized profusely for all the problems he caused and his actions, from cheating with one of my best friends right after we were married to his abuse towards me and his behavior in general. It was a letter for Marcus to lay out all his guilt and let me know he was better personally and unhappy in his current marriage. He wanted to visit me. It so happened that he told me he would be in Des Moines on some business trip. That sure felt like a flashing danger light and a big red flag. It's only a 90-minute drive from Des Moines to Iowa City. This was something I had to think about.

His email went on to explain that after I left, he went home to Indiana. He told his parents about everything that happened between us. They suggested that he attend anger management therapy. He did, or at least he told me he did. Then he had a story of how he went into the Navy at the age of thirty and worked in Special Operations on a submarine. While working on the sub, he was caught in an explosion, lost some of his eyesight, and had some other injuries. He was fine physically but had to wear glasses. Now, if you think that sounds like a movie plot, you are not alone. However, his dad told Perry these same things in the early 2000s. After all of that, he returned to Minnesota and his wife, the girl he had been seeing while we played there. That much I know was true. But, as he stated earlier, he was unhappy with his marriage. My first thought was that she was most likely the unhappy one in the marriage, but I kept that to myself.

Since his move back to Minnesota, he had been working as a manager at an Area Chamber of Commerce in a town with lots of parks and lakes. I was a little suspicious about his intention to see me, but I told him that if he was coming, he should meet me at my martial arts studio. I knew there would be lots of people around, so I felt much better in that situation.

He arrived while I was teaching a class. I didn't recognize him at first. As soon as the class finished, I went behind the big front desk, and he walked up to me and said that I looked exactly the same as I did in my twenties.

I told him, "Really? Thanks, how are you?"

Lame, I know, but I guess I didn't know what to say as I was busy checking my students out. He asked if we could go for dinner.

After all the students left and I closed the building, we went across from the studio to a crowded chain restaurant to catch up. My choice of the close-by crowded Chili's restaurant was on purpose. He was shaky, nervous, and couldn't eat a bite, which was very strange to me since I had never seen that type of behavior from him throughout the years we spent together. I was fine but couldn't figure out what was going on. It was like he was afraid of something as ordinary as just talking to me over dinner. This confused me, but I was figuring things out quietly while I observed him. As we left the restaurant, I remembered he was driving a large "company" van with no windows and no logo. He walked me over to the passenger side of that van and started to stutter as he tried to talk. This was an M.O. of a kidnapping, and instinctively I knew it. He had parked the van tightly next to my car since he followed me there. I was ready to leave, so we said our goodbyes and said let's be sure to keep in touch; and at that moment, he outstretched his arms to pull me in for a hug, but it looked like more of a grab. I didn't reciprocate as I felt my radar kick in. I unlocked my driver's side door only, slid in, and locked the doors.

I never heard from him again. But I do know that he realized, when he saw me after all that time, that I was always the one in control of myself, not him, no matter how hard he tried, and that I am still very much in control of my life. Although I did attempt to email him about a week later to thank him for the 23-year-old letter and for stopping on his way back to wherever he was headed, I heard nothing back. He was afraid of me. Imagine that. Later, I discovered that in 2006, he was arrested for embezzling from his job. I knew Marcus was dangerous, and I was satisfied that I hadn't heard back from him and was glad to hear that his wife divorced him for her safety.

Dangers can be anywhere, especially where you least expect them. Be aware of your surroundings and know how to defend yourself the best you can.

CHAPTER 9 – THE BEGINNING OF THE HOLIDAY ROAD BAND EXPERIENCE:

It's a Long Way Down the Holiday Road

"On the road again Just can't wait to get on the road again

The life I love is making music with my friends And I can't wait to get on the road again

On the road again Goin' places that I've never been

Seein' things that I may never see again I can't wait to get on the road again...

Like a band of gypsies, we go down the highway

We're the best of friends Insisting that the world keep turning our way

And our way" ~Willie Nelson

Photo courtesy of Mike Breazeale circa 1984-85

By the early 80s, Bruce and I left Rob's band, and together we dropped the band names that the management wanted us to use and got our musicians through the grapevine. The agents and management agreed to this since we were well-known and in demand. With our new drummer, Roger, and one of several bass players through the rotating door, we became Holiday Road Band, a name chosen by Roger, Bruce, and me from the movie "National Lampoon's Vacation". The names Shannon and Bruce were highly respected and known names in the business after all our touring and playing in hundreds of venues for thousands of people over the years. Roger was a well-known drummer from his Midwestern roots, had stints in Las Vegas show acts, as well as working as a dance instructor. Holiday Road Band was a highly sought-after road band that packed the houses and halls throughout the 1980s and early to mid-90s.

This was the first edition of Holiday Road Band. We continued to find players as needed from Oregon, Iowa, Pennsylvania, Florida,

Minnesota, Michigan, West Coast areas and other states. We kept on rolling over the highways from North to South and East to West, living in hotels and band houses and playing fifty weeks a year. We replaced our bass player several times due to strange circumstances each time but kept the configuration the same otherwise.

Dennis, our first Holiday Road Band bass player, was a guitar player. We went to see him play in Bemidji, Minnesota, to meet him and check him out. He had contacted us by phone through our agencies. Dennis was playing guitar with a decent band. He was very interested in joining us due to, you guessed it, friction in his current situation. He said yes to playing bass, so we agreed to rehearse and see how it went. Dennis did well with the bass and singing, but he had some antics off-stage that we tried to overlook, involving the usual; he was married with children and used his road life for girls, alcohol, etc. He was fun to be around and perform with, entertaining, but not a good musical match for the rest of the band. One of the things he did was to do a high front kick to Roger's ride cymbal during a couple of songs. Roger wasn't very happy with that move and let Dennis know.

After several months of working with Dennis, which in road band terms is the equivalent of several years, there was Dan from Northern Indiana. He was a solid enough player but refused to sing harmonies, leads, or anything else on stage, even though he was a fair enough singer. We would rehearse with him on harmonies, which worked fine at rehearsal, but in front of the audience, he would not sing. My gut instincts told me it was more than just being shy. I felt that he had depression issues or something similar. It turned out that it was a precise instinct. Dan always appeared to be quiet, solitary, and despondent. He spent all his off-stage time in his dark hotel room unless we were rehearsing or playing. He never opened the curtains in his room. He would only have one lamp on or just the bathroom light in his room, and he never changed out of his sweats unless it was for him to perform each night.

We invited Dan to go to dinner with us periodically and to go sightseeing with us when we were in Wisconsin where there was so much to see and do. He went along and was his usual quiet self, but at least he was smiling. Fresh air and sunshine can do wonders for the human soul. He didn't seem to have any traits of a drug user or otherwise and never had drugs with him or even alcohol. Eventually, Bruce and Roger were able to coax him to swim or throw the football and do other physical activities, and I caught him with that smile more than once. After having a heart-to-heart talk with him a couple of months later, he decided to head home and get help. I hope he did, and I hope he has lived a better life. He certainly deserves to find happiness. We really have fond memories of Dan.

We replaced Dan with a young guy named Gordon from Minneapolis, whom our agent for that area said was available. Buckle up; this story is quite a ride.

We went to pick him up in Minneapolis. He seemed very young, but we were promised he was old enough to work in the clubs. He appeared to have been living in a house with a group of college-age kids. We trusted our agents to find musicians the right age for where we played. Maybe it was not the best idea.

Gordon insisted on being called 'Flash'. He even had a big, bright lightning bolt on his guitar strap. It was a challenge working with Flash because he would only play what he felt like playing instead of learning the bass lines that were given to him for each song. That made the entire sound of the band loose and sloppy. He had no idea how to improvise or how to hear the way a good, strong bass line really leads the music. We were skeptical about his ability to play and wondered if he honestly had ever been with a professional group.

We had a band meeting to talk about tightening up the music since Flash was going off on his own while playing instead of following the music. Bruce and I tried to be kind in our critique and offered to help him learn the parts, that is, until he flipped back his long blonde hair and said,

"It's a matter of opinion, and it's up to my own interpretation as to what to play, like fusion."

"OK," I said, I see. Well, my opinion is that you're done after this week, so interpret that any way you like."

At this same time, our drummer and his wife (Roger and Cindy) had two of their daughters, aged eleven and thirteen, traveling with us during the summers. The girls were a little sad to see Flash go because they thought he was so cute, and they were highly entertained when he was practicing vocals in his hotel room. Why? Because he was loud, like nails on a chalkboard. The other guests thought it was some animal screeching. I'm not saying that to be mean, but it's true. The girls would hang out in the hallway by his door and giggle until he heard them open his door, and they had to run back to their room so he didn't see them. Yes, it was a pretty funny sight and sound.

Later we discovered that he was only seventeen and had lied about his age, among other things. We never let that story fade away. They still have vocal impressions of him that their own kids have now heard a few times or more. We drove 'Flash' back to his home after the week was over.

You have to crack a few eggs to make an omelet or a crack few nuts. Next up on the bass was Joe. This is a story that Roger, our drummer, and his wife, Cindy, still speak about today after all these years. Joe looked handsome and put together but seemed a little shady, and we couldn't pinpoint why we felt that way. We wanted to give him a chance since you never know. He had a girlfriend who would sit at the bar and hike her skirt up so men would talk to her and buy her drinks or proposition her and of course, she took the money instead of the drink. Her famous line was telling everyone that Joe, the bass player, is her boyfriend, almost like a warning or maybe a badge of honor, or, well, both. Joe and his girlfriend, who he picked up sometime somewhere in some town, and had asked her to travel with him, were ultimately an odd couple. I don't recall where they were from or where they went after we fired Joe.

Joe seriously could not sing. He was a proficient, qualified player but singing is another story. However, that's not why he was fired from Holiday Road Band.

One of the memories of Joe is that he wanted to sing George Michael's Careless Whisper. In my head, I was saying, OH HELL NO! But we decided to let him try it in rehearsals. It was not good, not at all. It was not even sung in the same key we were playing. We thought he would eventually hear himself and decide on his own not to do this song. He desperately wanted to sing it to his girlfriend, who, as you remember, he picked up at a gig somewhere along the way before joining us. She thought it was cool to be with a guy in a traveling band who would sing to her from the stage and live in his hotel room. We decided to let him try Careless Whisper one night early in the week. Sadly, I believe he heard himself sounding just like George Michael. After that, we told him we were sorry, but he would have to give up the song. He did and didn't sing again, which was no problem.

Holiday Road Band with Joe Circa 1984 Photo public domain

Oh wait, there's more.

One of our favorite venues to play, Barnabee's, was a wonderful place with great management who were very respectful of us as people as well as musicians. Sometimes, that's not the case when you are a full-time musician. We always drew big crowds and audiences at this venue and we had a good reputation.

This was the time when VCR's and VHS movies were new and exciting. Joe and his girlfriend decided to 'borrow' a VCR from the hotel desk (which was there for guests to rent). The hotel manager, Harv, whom we knew well and trusted, called us at our next gig and asked if we had accidentally packed the VCR with us. If you remember, VCRs were rather large and heavy, and we had our own that we traveled with. We said no, but we would check with the other band members.

As luck would have it, Joe and his girlfriend took it with them. They rented it for one night and just left town with it. When we saw it in their room at the new hotel in the next town, Bruce and I asked them if that was the VCR from the last hotel because we saw a couple of stickers they had pasted on the VCR that said Property of Joe. He told us that Harv, the manager at the Barnabees, had told them they could use it and bring it back when we returned in a few months, and they had put stickers on it so it wouldn't get stolen. Seriously? I don't think so. Bruce and I took the VCR. We called Harv, who said he wondered what had happened to it, and we shipped it back to him. Joe was asked to leave the band and take his girl with him. You can't make this stuff up.

That leads us to the best bass player. Jeff R. was (and is) a first-rate musician who can play any style of music easily, powerfully, and perfectly. He was easy to work with and had been traveling with a funk music band. We met him earlier during our days in Rob's band at a huge concert hall when we were the opening act for a well-known, at the time, country artist. Jeff R. was playing across the road at a funk and rock club. He came over to hear us during his breaks and we all hit it off well. We were able to get in touch with him since we had exchanged home phone numbers and asked if he was working with anyone at the time. He was happy and surprised to hear from us and decided to join us. Everything was smooth sailing for a long time. The band sounded the best we'd ever sounded and brilliantly solid. Jeff R. became family.

Holiday Road Band with Jeff R circa 1985 photo public domain and courtesy of Mike Breazeale

After many cities, towns, many miles, and many stages later, Jeff R. told us he would be leaving the road life and moving back to Pennsylvania. His wife was there, and even though he had formed another relationship during his road time, he wanted to go back to try and make it work with his wife. We were happy for him, and it was a calm parting. Jeff R. was and is an outstanding guy in every aspect, and we missed him. It's hard to find musicians and personalities like that. He still plays with his well-known, popular regional band in his hometown and state.

After Jeff R., there was Dave. Dave was a tight player with good vocals but had some strange and shifty ways. Shifty is the word I think best describes him. We kept wondering why he had so much equipment with him that he never really used, in addition to the equipment he needed and used for performances and maybe a backup bass or amp. He had no explanation other than he collected amps and other equipment from other bands that were selling or getting rid of or that they had given him. GIVEN HIM? Nope! Now, there's another flashing red light. No musician would give away an expensive amplifier, or any amplifier at all, much less travel with that much heavy equipment and lug it around.

Well, you guessed it. We discovered that Dave had been in several bands and had stolen property from them every time he left the bands. And he had been fired from several bands before we hired him. We have no idea about this until later. Of course, the agents didn't relay that information. We didn't have cell phones, but we did have connections. That's how we found out. We were in Northern Texas, and on the night that Dave was fired from our band, we heard fast footsteps outside our hotel room door after we had all gone to bed. Roger and Cindy heard it too. It was close to a run on the concrete walkway, passing by all the rooms. Roger jumped up and followed. It was Dave. Roger caught him as he tried to pry open the back doors to the band-van/bus and take an amplifier he felt was owed to him. Maybe as severance pay? As the saying goes, a leopard doesn't change its spots. I wonder if he was attempting to head out to another bass job with a new band because we put the word out, and the word among traveling bands is a trust that agents can't figure out.

After all that, the rest of us discussed the future of Holiday Road Band. Roger, our drummer, and his wife, Cindy, still two of my dearest and best friends, decided to take their daughters back home and try to settle in by joining a local group in the Des Moines area. The girls traveled with us in the summers and were getting closer to high school and graduation ages. We remain close friends, more like family. I found some old VHS and cassette tapes of all of us from the early 80's through the mid-90s. Including Dennis, Jeff R. and Jeff H. I'm putting them into digital files, and it has been so much fun seeing all of our antics and seeing us playing on different stages, the audiences, dancers, and the sights of the different locations. The skits Roger and Bruce did that always made us laugh out loud were Saturday Night Live worthy. I also found some VHS tapes from the days of Rob's band that Bruce's brother made of our performances.

At that time, I wanted to spend more time getting myself educated on other things I was interested in, which included several things I still do today. I had lots of books with me. It was unfathomable to waste my mind, energy, and time like I watched so many others do while living on the road to anywhere. How boring that seemed, and I couldn't imagine not keeping busy or exploring, hiking, reading, and filling my head with everything from physical fitness to the planets, the stars, astral projection to crystals and stones, to all those things that I've thought about in this Universe since I was a child. I reassured myself that I could keep progressing and that I had become wiser and expanded as I kept perfecting my talents. These are things that I would spend my entire life doing and practicing. I mentioned to my mom more than once that I wished I could have been there at the beginning of the Universe and still be there at the end of it. I remember her response was something like this: you have been, and you will be.

CHAPTER 10 – THEM CHANGES

And the Music Played On

"The first time I set eyes on you I listened to you sing, yeah, yeah

We didn't have to speak 'Cause the words said everything Yes, you walked right into my life And we were on our way, yeah

So long ago But it feels like yesterday

You still got that light in your eye (yes you do) And our day is comin' by and by

I'm traveling this long road to be with you

We still got a long way, we still got a long way to go.

Some of my best memories are days I spent with you, yeah

Each time we hit the road it was always somethin' new

We won't forget the days gone down They're written in our hearts, yeah yeah

And we're as much in tune as we were right at the start"

~Gerry Rafferty

In 1986, Bruce and I had decided that it would be a lot easier to try out some new technology to become a duo act that sounded like a full band after all the years of feeling responsible for band members, getting them to and from gigs, and their behavior. This was a brilliant idea and worked like magic. It meant we could do studio work or play smaller venues if we wanted and make more income.

In January, while in Tulsa, Oklahoma, and before changing what was the original Holiday Road Band, we found some brand-new computerized equipment at a progressive music store to help us accomplish this. The day we were heading to the store to purchase it, we decided to get up early and watch the Challenger launch. It launched us into another dimension. We, like everyone else around the world, could not believe what we had just seen. Just like the JFK and Bobby Kennedy shootings, it is forever etched in my brain. We couldn't wrap our heads around the horrific event or even begin to understand any of it.

After we could gather our thoughts, we went to that same Tulsa progressive music store and, with the help of the staff there, purchased everything we needed, including many MIDI devices, a drum machine, and a bass machine. We were trying to stay focused on how all this new equipment worked as the televisions in the store kept reporting all the news stories on the horrific Challenger explosion scene. I still feel the same way just writing this.

Our next move was to go to my mom's house in Houston for two weeks to program our set list songs and rehearse them with our fascinating new high-tech band. We tapped out all the drum parts on the drum machine and played the bass lines from the keyboard, which transferred to the bass machine. It was all recorded onto another machine to a small hard disk, and we could play our instruments and sing while the rest of the band was in the box. It was so advanced for the time, and we had the freedom to play any music we chose to play.

The next task was to explore and investigate the best agencies to work with in this capacity. Acclaimed agent and manager Marv Dennis in Nashville came highly recommended to us, and we also hired a manager in Minneapolis.

So, off we went to one of our favorite cities on Earth, Nashville, Tennessee, and met up with Marv Dennis. Marv took us around Nashville, introducing us to some big-name artists, some were his acts, some were represented by other management. Marv took us to see his acts like David Allan Coe. For the record, David Allan Coe is seriously larger than life. A giant grizzly bear of a man who had been in reform schools and prison for much of his earlier life. Besides the story of what put him in prison, most of us know him as a well-respected singer-songwriter. He appeared on stage in a gigantic red cape with fringe and an enormous eagle embroidered or painted on the back. When he came out to perform, he spun around so the cape was in full glory. What a stage presence he portrayed. Everyone behind the stage and his band seemed to shrink when he was on the stage. This was a tremendous way to experience Nashville and get booked for bigger and better gigs. Marv booked us around Nashville and the surrounding area under the name NightBird. He took us to recording studios, to all the music stores, introduced us to everyone, and made us feel appreciated for our talent and reputation.

The most unprecedented and spectacular place we were booked into was the Opryland Hotel (now called Gaylord Opryland Hotel and Resort). This place was a breathtaking city all on its own. It's changed over the years and is still one of the most sought-after places for visitors and artists to stay in Nashville.

There were so many restaurants and entertainment venues inside the hotel, mall-type stores with upscale clothing, jewelry, boots, glamorous shoes and dresses, and anything sparkly and eye-catching. The hallways and byways had beautiful art in glass displays. Three beautiful atriums with dancing lighted fountains and stages graced the inner circles of the building. While we were there, Liberace was in the largest atrium. He was magnificent as he glittered and sparkled like a million stars in the sky. His costumes, lighting, the fountains, and the stunning pianos were hypnotic.

We went to the atrium to see Liberace on just about every other break throughout each night. He was so kind and welcoming. We were there for several weeks, and we played six sets, seven nights a week. My feet hurt terribly, but the time flew by. Most gigs are three to four sets of music, five nights a week. This was a gem—exciting, full of light and music, wonderful people from all over the world every night, all night long, and no doubt unforgettable.

Joe Ferraro, another one of our regional agents from Minnesota, had lots of acts roaming the highways. He made it possible for all his acts to communicate with each other by recording a message onto a cassette tape and playing a song – original or otherwise. That made it so we could hear and almost see all of us waving to each other and being the first to hear any original songs we had to share. Afterward, he would make copies of the cassettes so we could all receive one each month, wherever we were at the time. This was, again, before any cell phones or the internet. We mailed our tapes back and forth so Joe could edit them into one cassette. Luckily, the World Wide Web was not far behind. Joe's method made for a close-knit group of musicians who respected each other and made longtime friends. I have no idea what most of these road warriors are up to these days, decades later, but I do keep in touch with a couple of them through email.

I don't know if other couples who have performed together every night for years had the same complications as Bruce and I had, but I would guess they did. The music always came first. Singing and playing together every night, feeling anger and frustration behind the stage some of those nights was the norm due to his drinking and other significant relationship problems it caused. Still, on stage, nothing could stop us from glowing at every performance and appreciating each other's talents. Living together 24/7 with a partner who has substance abuse problems and the great love between us caused emotions to run high. We found ourselves singing to each other and meaning the lyrics of some of those songs. We were always two independent people who, without question, depended on each other. One minute, we would be so furious and exasperated with each other that we felt consumed by it. Then, out of the exhilaration and joy of the music we were playing and singing, Bruce would say that he loved the way I sang a song, or how I sang a specific line of a song or the parts I was playing, and I knew he meant everything he said. And how he could play every instrument and sing so beautifully with ease and emotion. Our voices never stopped blending so effortlessly without trying, and even after all the nights we had sung together we never once doubted or dismissed our talents and our intense chemistry. We knew what it meant to share such a light in this world and tell each other how we felt when playing music together. I often think about all the musicians we encountered who were on some stage every night and still send them good vibes today.

There's more to this story, including the regrouping of Holiday Road Band in the early 2000s. But all that time in between is where we are going next in this story.

Shannon and Bruce 1989 Photo Public Domain

CHAPTER 11 – 70s through 90s INSTRUMENTS AND Technology

Advances to Help Musicians Advance

Playing ARP Omni Circa 1977

In my first years of performing locally, I purchased a Fender Rhodes keyboard. It was magical—the keyboard we heard in most 70s music. I had several of them, and each time a new model came out, I got it.

As my first band grew in the community and added more songs to the list, I added an Arp Omni and Moog Synthesizer and switched from a Fender Rhodes to a Wurlitzer Electric Piano in about 1974. This keyboard had only 64 keys and no adjustable legs. That made it tough to stand up and play since I was constantly bending and leaning over. I ended up using a chair until I found some newer stage technology. Google those keyboards, and you'll see them on some vintage synthesizer and keyboard museum sites.

Wurlitzer Electric Piano Circa 1974

Technology kept evolving and changing. My keyboards kept up with the times the best I could manage. My favorite 80s keyboard was my Yamaha Electric Baby Grand. It was a beast to travel with but magnificent in sound. The legs were adjustable but not quite high enough for me to play standing. Bruce, being a logical, creative brain, was a great puzzle and problem solver. He had a brilliant idea to set the legs and the sustain pedal on concrete blocks. Well, this made it just perfect! Except for one thing: the guys would have to lift one corner at a time to get it on the blocks for each stage. It was worth it.

That enormous but spectacular instrument came apart into two pieces: the harp (piano strings) and the eighty-eight-key keyboard. It was in a giant blue Anvil case on wheels. It had to be tuned periodically, so I learned how to do that from a good friend, piano tuner, and musician Jim, who lived in a town we frequented on the road.

Yamaha Electric Grand 1983

In the early to mid-80s, I added more synthesizers to my setup: an Ensoniq EPS and a Roland Juno 106. Around 1986 I replaced the monster Yamaha with a Korg EPS-1 String Machine Analog E-Piano (electric piano with a setting for string sounds). It didn't sound the same, but it was delightfully good nonetheless, and I got used to it quickly. The piano keys were weighted, so it felt like a piano.

Several of the synthesizers I used were various models of Roland keyboards, and without question, I loved those keyboards. After a couple of big robberies over the years in Houston, Tulsa, and Iowa City, which all musicians go through at least once, I decided to go back to using two Korg keyboards. They are still my favorites, and I am completely satisfied with the sound and quality every time I hit those keys.

Microphones have evolved over the years, too. I have one favorite. If anything ever happens to it, I will get the same model again.

Microphones enhance our personal instrument of voice. They are used for different purposes on stage too, like using a microphone on an amplifier to enhance and project the sound of an instrument like a guitar or keyboard, and there are specific types for that use.

My acoustic/electric and electric guitars have also changed over time. My ultimate favorite electric/acoustic is a beautiful, rich, and full-sounding Taylor Cocobolo wood guitar. My favorite electric guitar is a royal purple Fender Stratocaster that has always been the apple of my eye. Yes, I still have those guitars.

My perfect Taylor Cocobolo guitar

Why is am old white tambourine from 1975 my most prized possession? That well-loved, hard-driven, old-fashioned tambourine was my constant companion from the time I bought it until the early 2000s.

Marcus and I were wandering about in a Louisville music store in 1975, and I saw it! Have you ever seen something that you knew had to be yours? That one beautiful dress, that pair of earrings, those shoes? You know what I'm talking about here. Imagine being a 21-year-old girl, already a lifelong musician/singer, walking into a music store and seeing the most spectacular bright white, most perfect tambourine on the planet, with jingles that were so shiny they sparkled like stars. It was as if the angels sang, the violins played, and the lights beamed down on it, and it sang to me all at the same time.

That tambourine made me feel almost supernatural. I adorned it with silk purple flowers and hung it from my mic stand and piano. I had a case just for that piece and packed it safely for travel. It's been everywhere I've been, from Florida to Canada and from the West Coast to the East Coast. It is more than just a common piece of music equipment. It has many stories to tell. And every time I see it hanging in my home office, I am taken away to other times and other eras of my life. It has never let me down.

I stopped using it in the early 2000s because I got a newer, smaller tambourine and wanted to be sure nothing ever happened to my first bright white circular rhythmic friend. It had acquired a crack, and the crack went all the way through. But you can't see that crack unless you are looking for it. There is a perfect break in a straight line across the handle. That doesn't mean it's done. It is just retired to a place of honor. It's never lost one jingle, although they are rusty. It's never lost its color, and it's happy.

It went home with me the day I first saw it, and the only time it had left my sight since that day in 1975 was when it was on display at the

IA Rock and Roll Hall of Fame when I was inducted into the Hall of Fame for Women Who Rock in 2016. After my Induction ceremony, I requested to take it back home since I was donating other items.

My prized tambourine

The Real Keys to the Highway

All those years on the road playing music full-time and living in hotels means that I have a huge collection of hotel room keys. It's amazing to see how a simple thing like a hotel room key has changed from 1977 to the 1990s (and today, of course).

In the earlier days, hotel room keys were big and heavy. Then, as technology entered, so did flat key cards. They looked like credit cards and were nothing like the old metal keys. I kept them all.

We learned songs from recordings. It all started with a crate of record albums and a record player that we took on the road with us in 1977.

Moving the record needle to review and get the lyrics written down on a notepad was the norm but not the easiest way. Hauling around record albums appeared to cause massive and tricky maneuvers while trying to keep them safe.

We also had cassette tapes, which were much easier to use. We recorded ourselves every night on a small boom box to see what we might need to rehearse. Most of those cassettes are in my possession, and I'm in the process of making them digital files. Surprisingly, using a boombox on a table in the middle of the audience gave us excellent, clear recordings.

In the early 80s, we were right there when MTV previewed. We learned about recording television shows and movies with a VCR and of course, we bought one. I remember the one we decided on had a removable part to attach to a video camera. We could not believe how heavy that equipment was. We were renting video cameras everywhere we went, which was beginning to be a hassle, so, of course, our next purchase was the camera. That VCR cost us around $1500, and I have since forgotten the cost of the camera because cameras kept updating and getting smaller, so of course we had to have the newest model. It was a lot of money, but we needed it. VCRs have been available since the late 70s, but then we could record anything, anywhere with our camera. I have so many VHS tapes from that era and am transferring those to digital MP4 files and the cassette tapes to MP3 files. The quality is not so good after thirty to forty years of being stored in a gym bag from place to place, but it is so much fun to see us in our twenties and thirties making the scenes.

Between 1977 and the 1980s our "home away from home" setup grew and changed. We didn't travel lightly. Eventually, we had a small dorm room-type refrigerator after getting smart and ditching the old coolers and ice. We had a small microwave, a hot plate, exercise equipment, cassette tapes, and our first computer, which was an Atari. It was pretty much a gaming system, and Bruce wanted something he could learn to program. So, we searched all the stores and got an Amiga. We decided to try a Tandy computer that seemed to be highly popular and got good reviews after seeing one in a Radio Shack. Bruce was sort of a tech geek so that eventually led us to finally getting a Commodore 64. We kept that forever. I still had it after he passed. Where is it now? It got water damage in a basement flood, and I was so sad to say goodbye to our old friend the Commodore 64.

While figuring out computers, each time we moved to a new hotel, we hooked up the system, learned how to use it, and got on CompuServe, which was one of the first email and chat services. (Who remembers that?). It was magical and unbelievably cool to be able to talk online to other people who were still up at 3 a.m. every night/morning. We spent hours talking to other traveling musicians and new people in chat rooms in other parts of the USA. We thought that was the most amazing thing ever.

I vividly remember going into an electronics store somewhere in Western Texas. An employee latched onto us and took us to a different part of the store to show us something brand new. He said, "Look at this!" He told us that this thing was going to change the way we listen to music. It was a Compact Disc. That disc was shiny and had lots of rainbow colors reflecting. The salesman threw the disc to the floor and ran his fingernail over it. He told us they were called

CDs and were indestructible. It's how cassette tapes were going to be replaced. We were very intrigued, and now we would start buying CDs and a CD player. We had a Walkman, which was replaced with a Discman. Then DVDs hit the market. And, as we have all learned, they are not indestructible, but at the time, were the most incredible high-tech things we ever saw.

Now, all we needed was streaming and downloading. Technology has changed majorly in an incredibly short time. Bruce would have loved the technology of today. He would have wanted it all and learned it all—computers, phones, smartwatches, and smart appliances.

CHAPTER 12 – MOVING TO IOWA CITY

A New Life and Reinventing Us

After several years of living on the road, Bruce's alcoholism was hitting new highs. The first thing he would do in a new town before we even checked into our hotel was to go to a local liquor store where he would purchase a large bottle or a gallon jug of vodka to have for the week if it lasted that long. This started to become a routine event in 1988 and forward. When we met, and for many years after, he would typically order whiskey and cola during the night and sometimes in the afternoon. It was an issue for me, but when the vodka became an everyday thing for him, his health was becoming critical. It felt crucial to understand it all.

When we moved to Iowa City, after his coma and recovery in Oklahoma in early 1993, his excessive drinking seemed to stop and start but never entirely stopped for any discernable length of time.

We left the road life because Bruce had become terminally ill. We moved to his hometown of Iowa City, which had become a second home for me, too, since about 1983. After moving, we got to know the local music scene and musicians and played many places in the Iowa City/Cedar Rapids area until Bruce's illness caught up with him for good, and he was in the hospital more than out.

When Bruce was better, we could play music live, and he even wrote songs again. He spent time drawing and always drew creatures and landscapes he said were from his home planet. I believe he, indeed, might have been here just visiting Earth. He had always drawn and was very artistic as his drawings included planets and creatures. From the day we met, he was highly interested in the Universe and the Solar System. There was a lot of back and forth, as he would be more functional for several days or even weeks, and then things turned around just like those weeks had never happened.

Bruce, the kid magnet circa 1994

It always felt like such a short amount of time before he derailed again. I was shriveling inside. I worked hard not to let this circumstance swallow me up. I kept myself occupied, busy, and upbeat for the most part.

At first, he seemed to be happy being alcohol-free. He attended AA meetings regularly; he went to rehab several times in different facilities and felt that he was accomplishing something. But each time it was short-lived, and drinking started again. I believed he was afraid to actually stop not knowing how life would be if he did.

I was becoming highly frustrated and angry. I was raging inside and so tired of smelling it and experiencing how it was affecting him and me. Smelling someone who is alcoholic is unavoidable since we sweat, we breathe, and everything we ingest comes out of our body in one way or another. The skin of an alcoholic person smells like a bottle of vodka or gin. Then, as it progresses, the skin and the eyes turn a sallow yellow.

He hid bottles everywhere around the house: under and behind stacks of towels in the linen closet, in the basement, and in the back of kitchen cupboards. He couldn't even have a glass of water without vodka in it. It was utterly mind-blowing to me. I could not understand how this got so out of hand. Sometimes, he would say that he wanted to stop for good, and the next thing he would say is that he never pictured himself living past forty. He was forty-four when he passed.

As I mentioned, the very unnatural odor of someone with this affliction is unmistakable and noxious, and the mental issues related to it, especially in a person I love and was so connected to, being so entirely self-destructive, is unfathomable. I was constantly spinning in circles. I was still working every day and could focus on something else. Why didn't I do anything about this? I did. I tried many things like throwing away the bottles that I found and searching for AA meetings and therapy for him. At times, I thought I was helping, but as I look back, I was starting to become codependent. Codependent. I had heard that term a million times but decided to research it to understand it completely. As soon as I figured it out, I tried to pull myself out of the rabbit hole, but it seemed like I couldn't.

We went to bookstores and wandered to the self-help section. I hoped that he would become interested in books that would help him. He did take an interest in helping himself and tried some of those books. The book that helped him the most was one he received from his AA sponsor. Unfortunately, nothing helped for very long. It just wouldn't stick. I could not understand since he knew the consequences of this lifestyle. Sometimes, I would see a glass of ice water sitting on the kitchen windowsill. When you have lived with this for such a long time, you're always aware, or maybe I should say suspicious of everyday things, so I smelled it. My heart sank, and I felt a flush of heat and dread come over me because it was vodka. Why does anyone think vodka has no smell? It began once again. This happened more times than I can count, so I didn't.

He was never going to be eligible for a liver transplant at this rate. And the complete truth is that he desperately wanted a transplant to happen. His primary liver specialist was a rude, bitter man who always seemed noticeably angry and frustrated with his patients. I can only imagine that seeing people like this every day had a way of making that doctor hardened. The way he was threatening and disciplining patients in a harsh, grim, and rigid way had the opposite effect.

It was like the school principal who gives a student stringent discipline, and the student never learns anything except that the principal doesn't care about helping him or believes that strict discipline is the only thing the student will understand. It's a form of mental games and abuse, and it never works. One day, that same liver specialist asked me why I was still with Bruce. His voice was cold and very matter-of-fact, and he spoke without thinking. It struck me as very odd and none of his business. I looked him straight in the eye and asked him if he would abandon someone he loved, like his wife or children or another family member, because they had a disease and needed help and you couldn't be inconvenienced or be there to watch it happen. The doctor bowed his head and never spoke that way to me again. This doctor had lost all compassion in his field and didn't appear to care. But it was still a fact that Bruce was not going to be on the liver transplant list until he could stay clean for six months.

During the times he was doing better, we had good days together. We worked and practiced our martial arts techniques and watched television shows we liked at two and three in the morning on weekends because those were the routine hours from our life before, and we were comfortable with those hours. Those times lasted as long as he could manage to take better care of himself.

The trips to the hospitals and emergency rooms were a way of life among all the other duties I had to do daily. Many of the trips to the hospital for Bruce were to get the fluid drained from his belly. What a horrific process to witness, not to mention for anyone to go through. I won't explain the process fully, but it involves a giant hypodermic needle and syringe through the belly button and filling several one-liter glass bottles. Sometimes, they drained enough yellow fluid to fill seven to ten of those bottles. When a liver isn't functioning, it cannot process many things, so the fluid stays in the body and must be drained out manually.

Bruce was unwaveringly kind and patient with the medical staff, and I was always very firm with the doctors and residents, and I was sure to let them know if they were judging him. I explained to them who he was and what his life had been like before this. Most of them already knew us from our music and that he had a disease, which substance abuse like alcoholism is classified as. Unfortunately, it is still such a stigma. I was powerful and direct during this time, and no one messed with me, but they respected me. The doctors, especially the residents, were somewhat nervous and timid when they saw me coming down the hallway and I liked it that way.

I can only hope that I finally got through to some of them. I felt them all step aside, seeming to 'part the seas' when I came to his floor and room. They made an effort to speak to me with dignity, which I fully expected.

This is very much a disease that is bigger than the person it affects, and at that time the specialists told me it was probably genetic from recent research they had been doing.

There had been some studies proving this theory, and since Bruce was an adopted person, no one knew for sure. Medical records were not part of the adoption process in the late 50s when he was adopted as a baby. Adoptions were clouded in secrecy with the understanding that their adoption records would remain sealed for life. During this era, adoption files rarely have any medical history on birth parents and even less regarding mental illnesses or similar histories. Indeed, info on birth mothers, in general, tends to be brief to nothing more than a name and date of birth for the baby, and info about the birth fathers was even briefer. In the 1950s, women giving their babies up for adoption were, apparently, under no constraints to identify the father. Often, they did, but it also was not unusual for a birth mother to refuse to identify the father, even if she knew him, and that decision was respected by social workers at the time. Bruce was born in 1957 and adopted at three months of age, fitting right into this category.

Bruce was very much loved and wanted. He was raised by wonderful parents, who had adopted his older brother a year or two previously. He was a kind, intelligent artist of all things and had a logical, mathematical mind. We discussed at length who he was and where he might have come from. Was alcoholism in his DNA? His liver specialists said it probably was since, at that time, there was new research and evidence that in cases like this, it was most likely genetic, as I mentioned before, and we believed this to be true.

During Bruce's final months on this planet, he wanted to find out. We researched DNA testing, and we could have it done, but it was very expensive at that time, and Bruce was afraid he would hurt his parents by doing this. So, he decided against it.

Those times when he was home from the hospital, he couldn't be left alone. I had to go to my day job so I could not stay with him all the time, every day. I never knew what would happen when Bruce was left alone at home during the day. On one midweek day, I took him to his mom's house while I went to work. She had offered, and so we went. And it was extremely hard for her. I am sure she did not understand the severity of his dementia. She had never had to experience anything like that, and it was like a jolt of reality that she didn't want.

He was on fourteen different medications, more than once daily. He had to take them at certain times. She had not seen this part of it for any length of time until that day, only in the hospital. Partly because, in her mind, he was fine and getting better so he would live for years, and partly because I didn't tell them everything that was going on since Bruce didn't want them to know as he assumed it would be very hard for his family. I never misled them to think that he was eventually going to recover. But I didn't fill them in on a lot of the specifics. Partly because he didn't want them to know and partly because I didn't like people to pity his situation or mine, it was just reality. And I was on my own for the most part.

His dementia was starting to become more pronounced.

Bruce had been walking down the street after unofficially leaving the hospital. He just walked out of the hospital. No one saw him or stopped him if they did see him. It was July and hot. He was walking around town in the middle of the afternoon with his heavy winter coat on and looking much like an unaccompanied escapee from a mental facility. The hospital notified the police, they called me, and I went to pick him up. He said he was walking home. This happened on more than one occasion in a couple of different circumstances. Another night, around 4:30 a.m., he called me from his hospital room telling me that something was going on in his room that wasn't right. He told me that they were trying to keep him held down and someone was attempting to tie him to his bed. They were also putting something strange in his food. And that monkeys were jumping around the room and trying to get into bed with him. He asked if I could please come and get him. I knew none of this was happening. I told him to ask the nurse if something was going on. He was afraid to do that. So, I asked him to go to sleep, and I would see him in a few hours. That seemed to work. He seemed fine when I went to the hospital that morning before I went to work, which was a relief. The staff had secured him to a locked floor, not to his bed, which meant he was free to roam the halls, but he couldn't leave that floor as the doors were locked. That made me feel much safer for him.

There were days when he was at home and not in the hospital when he called me several times a day while I was at work. Every time he called it was a hallucination or something that was coming after him. Once, he called to tell me a cat had gotten into the house and was trapped inside a pillow. We had no cats or dogs. Bruce tore that pillow apart and set out some water and food for the cat. He told me he cut open the pillow to let the cat out so it could breathe, and it was hiding somewhere under the furniture. He thought leaving food and water for it would coax it to come out. I left work and rushed home to see if this was at least a tiny bit true. I found the torn-up pillow and Bruce looking under the sofa and chair and calling for the cat. Of course, there never was a cat trapped inside a store-bought pillow or even a cat in the house at all.

As the days passed, he appeared wasted, smaller, more fragile, weak, older, and had a pronounced yellow color. Yellow, like a cheap tanning lotion, with a little bit of a greenish tint. The whites of his eyes were the same color. Our friend Kris, who was our hair stylist came to see him in the hospital. She was lovely. She came to his room to give him a haircut, hoping it would make him feel more normal. He was so happy, and she was in tears. It was a good thing for him and her as well. She had never really known the whole situation. I thank her to this day for that gesture of complete and unabridged kindness.

When 9/11 happened, Bruce was literally living at the hospital on a liver patient floor. He accepted it like it was his new apartment or condo. He had been in a procedure that morning and wasn't able to see the horrifying events of the day. I was there when he was waking up to TV news.

"Did you see this"? He asked.

I filled him in on whatever details I knew about 9/11 up to that point. To help someone understand him, Bruce was a very diverse human. There was never a person he wouldn't give the shirt off his back to and give his last five dollars. We all want to be welcoming and receiving to all humans, well, most of us, anyway. Bruce was the epitome of these actions and never questioned anyone or thought of any person to be something different than human, after all. He championed all cultures.

He was always very respectful and friendly to the entire hospital staff, even those staff members who caused my instincts to scream out loud in frustration. His birthday, October 2, 2001, would be his last. The nurses on duty that day gave him a birthday cake and allowed him to leave his room to go outside. He asked if he could go to a store to purchase some things to have in his room and come right back. I would take him and bring him back. The two nurses he spoke to told him they would turn around and not see him leave the hospital grounds. He lit up like it was the best day ever, and we went on a short little shopping expedition for toiletries so he could feel cleaner and more comfortable. He couldn't walk well, so he was excited to use a motorized shopping cart; it was technology for him. He played with it up and down the aisles, backing up and turning around, just like a kid with a new bike. This was a good and happy time since he was living there at the hospital and had not been outside for such an extended time, except to go to the patio in a wheelchair. When we returned, everyone had some birthday cake. This was his last birthday on this planet. He would not want anyone to feel sorry for or pity him.

During his illness, he repeatedly told me, "This would make me happy," and "If I only had that."

He wanted computers, laptops, DVD players, something, anything to do with technology. He was not allowed to have a cell phone at the hospital, or he would have had one. I tried my best to find a lot of these things, but instead of thinking about it, I'm afraid I was being co-dependent again. I was working full-time, being a caregiver for someone that I was always afraid to leave alone because he would take off walking or try to hurt himself or worse. I had also been running my Taekwondo and Fitness Academy and working full-time. It felt like having five or six full-time jobs. My debt soared because of everything he swore would make him happy. In the end, I had to file for bankruptcy to save myself from $103,000 of debt. I had no other option. That's the co-dependency aspect. Was it all worth it? I have to say the part that was worth it all is the fact that I learned so much from all the multitudes of events in those ten years. I look back and feel like I lived a lifetime learning things I would use later in life or at least be able to help someone else.

And so, it all comes down to the beginning of the last day.

CHAPTER 13 – FINDING ME AND MORE

Her Town Too

"It used to be her town, It used to be her town too

Well, people got used to seeing them both together

But now, he is gone, and life goes on

Nothing lasts forever, oh no" ~JD Souther, James Taylor

Photo by Mike Breazeale Circa 2006

Bruce was a genius musician and a gentle, kind man who could never find what it was that he was looking for, so he had become a substance abuser and didn't know why. It started early in his life. He told me his parents kept a bottle of wine in a cabinet for guests because his parents didn't drink. His taste for it started at age twelve when he decided to test out that bottle. As he grew into his teen years and experimented with other substances, it just developed into a way of life. As time passed, and in the music world, which was his world, it was easier to find and get anything he wanted. I can remember throwing drugs down the toilet and telling him we couldn't be together if the pills and cocaine continued. The drugs finally stopped for the most part, but the alcohol continued.

After all the years of rock/pop notoriety on the road with Bruce, my world changed overnight. I moved to Iowa to become his caregiver because he had become extremely ill. This is where his family was. It wasn't so bad at first compared to what it morphed into later because Bruce was getting better when we first returned to Iowa City. We played our music a lot locally, went back to the martial arts and boxing from our youth, and moved up in ranks, all the while knowing that was not the life we were meant to be in. We made more musician friends from all over the area as we played regularly. My passion for fitness, martial arts, and boxing led to owning a martial arts/fitness studio as a fourth-degree Blackbelt, which led to more and more of my life in the fitness community as a professional trainer in weight training and boxing, especially for women.

I always considered my full-time "day job" at the University to be supplemental and unimportant, but since I had to pay bills, that's what I did. I never let my dreams die (although they seemed to be sleeping for a bit) and was never afraid to do exactly what I needed and wanted to do simultaneously. Even though I realized that I loved every second of being back into martial arts and the boxing ring, it didn't feel altogether fitting. I accepted the fact that I was still doing things I loved, then looked at the situation and what I had gained from taking on that challenge.

The music played on. Bruce got worse. Alcohol turned into Hepatitis C and liver disease, which turned into liver cancer.

In 1991, only a few years before this move, a physician friend of ours and fan, Alan, in Gulf Shores, Alabama, where we played regularly, told Bruce that if things didn't change, his life expectancy would be about ten years. That doctor was spot on. Exactly ten years after that diagnosis, Bruce passed away from his illness in 2001, and I was left with the freedom of choice and trying to find out what I wanted and also to remember who I was before the caregiving years.

Something as simple as going to the grocery store made me stop and think. I would always be sure to get the things that Bruce liked and would/could eat like his favorite yogurt flavors, soups, and the foods that would be good for him and easy to eat and easy on his stomach. When we moved to Iowa City, he was told by his doctors that he had so many ulcers that his stomach looked like raw hamburger meat from the alcohol abuse.

It was an unfamiliar feeling as I headed over to the yogurt section and then stopped myself. I could make the decisions on what to get, and I could decide what I wanted to fill my refrigerator with. That took some getting used to. Those simple things that were habitual just changed in a flash, and I had to tell myself that it was fine and not selfish.

When some time had passed, and 2001 turned into mid-2002, the first thing I did was put it all away in my memory and get out my guitars to find myself again. Not that this wasn't part of who I had always been, but I needed to remember where I came from.

I chose to pick up my guitars, set up my keyboards, and also pulled out some old exercise videos to rewire my brain. I played songs I remembered from the past, songs I wanted to learn, new music from Sheryl Crow, and my favorite songs from Linda Ronstadt and other artists I love. I set up a small recording studio in one of the offices of my Martial Arts and Fitness Academy. I spent countless hours recording multi-instruments and harmonizing vocals with myself. It was just what I needed. Sometimes, I would be in my studio until after 2 a.m. because I had lost track of time and wanted to keep singing and producing my recordings.

I played a few solo gigs. It was great fun and well-received, but it didn't feel the same; something was missing. What else could I do to make this new life feel fulfilling?

I renewed my personal training education and bought the Martial Arts Academy from the Korean family that owned it. I taught adults and children Taekwondo classes five days a week and fitness classes three days a week. I added three other Martial Arts practices and added a yoga instructor.

This led to being part of who I am now, but a lot of "stuff" swallowed up the decade of my forties so that decade is all a blur of caretaking and trying to move forward. I was forty-seven when Bruce passed.

During that time, I worked that 9-5 job which was tough to do when I used to work the other 9-5, and I loved that life, inside knowing it was the only thing I ever wanted to do. When we moved into the new life, I didn't even know what to wear for an office type of job. With help from friends, I was able to dress for the job I had but never wanted. I was working at a medical clinic and every day, every single time I walked through the hallways there, my mind couldn't conceive or believe I was in this position. "What am I doing"? I asked myself many times during the day. It felt like I was shrinking.

Growing into that new lifestyle, I met many new people who have become lifelong friends. I wouldn't change that for anything, as our lives must change throughout the years as we learn and evolve.

After several years in that arena, I quit the higher-paying job that seemed to drag me down more and more and took a management position in a large, world-renowned music store. It was better, and it was, at the same time, not so great. The positive part was that two of the musicians I knew from those early 80s were working there, and it was a great surprise to see them. The not-so-great part was management with big-shot egos, an issue we all had to deal with. However, I could travel to the other satellite stores and interact with the employees, music teachers, and students who were taking lessons, and eventually, that led me to become the coach for the Weekend Warriors program, which is a program/workshop for adult and teen musicians who are looking for a way to get started or get back into playing and performing with other musicians, much like a school of rock. It was a fantastic way to help local musicians who wanted to play in a group again find each other, and I just loved how it enhanced the self-esteem and talent of the musicians as I used my experience and talents to help them. Some of the musicians and temporary bands from those days are still together.

One thing leads to another. Through leading that program, I met my current guitarist, Walter, who has been with me since 2003, and also Ken and Allison, a drummer who was with me for over a decade with his fantastic wife on backing vocals and other incredible musicians. I was also asked to write a monthly music article for Making Music Magazine out of Syracuse, New York, in the early 2000s, which I truly loved. I wrote articles each month for Making Music Magazine until I left the music store job in 2004.

Iowa City is a city of world-famous writers, musicians, and movie-makers. There was always something to explore and something new and exciting to do. I just had to keep finding what it was that I wanted to make happen.

The new edition of Holiday Road Band began in 2003, precisely 20 years after the original Holiday Road Band, which was sheer coincidence, or was it?

Putting Holiday Road Band back together with my current bandmates, including my brilliant guitarist, Walter, who has been with me since the beginning of this new configuration, was the best thing I could have done. In 2003, the band reformed with new members including Walter, our original drummer Roger, his wife, Cindy, and another revolving door of ever-changing bass players, until we finally added our current much accomplished and brilliant bass player in 2010.

It seems like a full cycle from 1983 to 2003 for me and Holiday Road Band. After Roger and Cindy left to go back home, they decided to move to Florida several years later. We added drummer Ken and his wife, Allison. They spent over a decade with us, which was such a wonderful time in the history of this band, until they moved to a city farther away for their work. We added a sharp, tight drummer who has been with us since 2016. Allison comes in to sing back up when she can. It feels good again. These people feel like family and have since day one.

HRB 2023-24

We are still growing and loving the music we play. When we became Holiday Road Band in 1983, we were a highly sought-after road band, packed houses and halls throughout the late 70s, 80s, and early 90s. The names Bruce and Shannon were well-known and genuinely respected names in the business even before 1983.

I lived the gypsy life for almost two decades. I left home to travel in January 1977 and met Bruce in 1980. We stayed together as a couple until his passing. That means we had twenty-one years together, good and bad. It was a life well-lived and well-loved, and Holiday Road Band is still in Iowa City and the surrounding areas.

The events that brought me here were destined to happen. This is the place I call home, and it feels that way. I came to live here in the mid-90s and stayed.

In 2016, I was inducted into the IA Rock and Roll Hall of Fame for Women Who Rock. Accolades follow, such as "Having been around for decades, all over the USA and Canada, Shannon's voice has been called "haunting," "emotional" and "gritty." People pull their chairs up to watch the lead guitar player, Walter." (~Radio Personality Boston Mike Ryan).

Over the years, I have strived to have higher education in physical fitness, nutrition, and antiaging, and I teach many group classes in weight training, kickboxing, and other fitness realms. I have many remarkable, dedicated personal training clients who get stronger with a better quality of life every week. Boxing and mixed martial arts are still my favorite wheelhouse of all, even though I have had some joint replacements due to the stress on my body from all the years on the road, standing and dancing around in high-heeled boots for five hours or more a night, lots of ankle rolls, and more recently high impact styles of the arts. But I still wouldn't change a thing. I am moving my body normally with lots of strength and making others happy and active every day.

Being increasingly interested in people's behavior, I trained to become a practitioner of a non-tranced-based hypnotherapy system developed in the U.K. that has been uncommonly effective in a short time. Change is inevitable, but sometimes, we need a little leap of faith to jump over the fence. I love this system and how it works to change lives.

Only two men have been in and out of my life since 2003. I never felt thoroughly comfortable with either of them and wanted the shelter of my own home, cherishing my solo time. These men had the same characteristics as the men I encountered at a younger age. Those who were narcissistic and controlling and not anyone I wanted to be with for any length of time or would be happy with. One of them attempted to move into my house. Before I knew it, he sold his house and moved into my small house with all of his clothes, boxes of whatever, and various things. It was too much. Crowding me. Controlling me, or trying to. Suddenly, there was no room to walk from one room to the next. There wasn't one minute when I was happy during this time except for my band. That was a mentally confusing time for me. After a time, he moved back out. I could not share my space with someone who tried to control my life. He pushed me not to have band rehearsals at my house, to get rid of my pets, and wanted to build onto the house I was living in and didn't even own. I vetoed every so-called suggestion. This went on way too long, but I didn't know exactly what to do. As soon as I found out he was secretly (and not so secretly) with someone else, I told him he had to move out. The next one was very short-lived. He was a womanizer and a phony. It was easy to see, but I waited too long. I realized I desperately needed to set boundaries for this new and different way of life.

Then, in 2011, Mike G. came into my life through fitness, friends, and music. He is a calm, gentle man who loves the fact that I am independent and strong and do my own thing without him feeling threatened. He has never controlled me or tried to change anything about me. I feel respected as a person, as a woman, and seen as a partner. The sensuality is back. To know what type of partner a person will be to you, watch how they treat their mother. Mike G. is kind and helpful and is the role model for all of this. And should be teaching a class to men about the subject of women. He grew up with four younger brothers, who are all exceptionally good men. They are all kind, outstanding givers, and thoughtful humans. I hope that we learn from each other every day. And the first time we hugged, I knew it was right. So, you see, I am sincerely blessed again, and my life is different, but truly fulfilled.

Mike and Shannon 2016

CHAPTER 14 – THE AFTER BUT NOT THE ENDING

Still Got a Long Way to Go

Getting married and having kids was never on my bucket list, and I've always been entirely satisfied and serene living alone. The music—singing and playing—was my one constant aspiration, and nothing would ever stop me from making it happen. At this time of my life, I am happy and busy, doing those things I am passionate about and helping others. It took most of my life to get here. Life has to move forward.

I'm not one to carry trauma or let it rule me because I always believed that those moments were all temporary roadblocks. I never gave up or gave in because I believed in my dreams and goals. I just didn't put a tag on them; it's just what I did, what I was always meant to do. However, I am someone who could never truly understand why people say and do things that would cause hurt, make fun of, and destroy the confidence of others. I have seen and experienced a lot of mistreatments, not only to myself but to others that seemed so unnecessary.

All that time on the spellbinding, vibrating, and undulating highway in the glow of the headlights and the blinding stage lights blazing in my eyes, it all seemed so easy then, even when it wasn't always so easy, it was worth every second. Time passed so fluidly that we never even noticed. It didn't fly by; it went slowly, smoothly, and anticipatory as if for a child who keeps asking,

"Are we there yet?

Through hazardous driving at times, abuse, laughter, days in the sun, days in the snow, anger, all the loading and unloading, our interesting and unusual fans and friends, amusing, all those temperamental and impressive musicians. Nothing seemed insurmountable, and difficulties didn't feel too difficult. Every puzzle had pieces that fit together to make a solution without even realizing how hard we tried because it just worked. It's much like the lyrics of a great song. And if I had a few secret trysts with more than one of the more famous folks we came across it's part of the life, opportunity, and freedom of the wind and the road.

Everywhere we went, there was incredible scenery, from soft white sandy beaches and clear turquoise oceans to the forest greens to several feet of snow with drifts taller than the bridges we drove over and under and every landscape in between. There were always wonderful, kind, adoring fans and friends, some who are still in our lives and some who left us too soon.

Nothing remains the same; it isn't supposed to, and those who force sameness will be unhappy. The Universe gives you chances to advance your life. If you fight it, the Universe will push you into it anyway. Go with the changes, especially the ones you don't expect, and find your own peaceful space. If you are unhappy and not comfortable with who you are, find a way to get there. It's worth everything, especially letting the right people into your life and heart and following your instincts; you have them for a reason. In these moments, many lose sight of their blessings. Their thoughts and energy can shift from a state of blessings and abundance to a state of lack. Their happiness can be easily derailed by any small negative thought or idea if you spend too much time on it. No one is immune to slipping out of gratitude, either. And if that happens, you're paying the price in your career, health, wealth, and relationships.

It can be hard to stay grateful all the time. But I want to remind you that no matter how unstable and challenging to maneuver your life can be, it's much easier than you think to keep improving and refining every aspect of your life with wisdom, kindness, and care. Simply. Because there is always something new on the other side of all of it, something you never expected and something better, or maybe just different but good. Be open, be ready. What legacy will you leave?

Sometimes, things get in the way of "living," but that's part of it all, too. To do what you want to do, you must sometimes do what you need to do. I never even considered compromising my ethics and self-respect in any situation. When you have been raised to be independent and to live your passions, your soul has been learning not to hurt others or yourself. Awareness is what happens. Awareness of how others may treat you. That's when you decide how you want to be treated and never turn back. You become aware of your surroundings to find safety, solace, and awareness of your mind and body.

The more I saw, the less I knew, which is still true today. And if you look at your own life, your travels, your people, your tribe, and where you've been, where you are, and where you came from, you will have much the same conclusion. Your age doesn't matter; your will does.

If you lose your soulmate, instead of dwelling on the past and the loss and wondering how you will ever be happy again or how you will get through your own life, discover the lessons that soulmate was here to teach you. Then you will see the light, the path that is open for you to travel, wherever it may lead. Know that there are opportunities and other soulmates just waiting in the wings and looking for you, too. Be open. You'll see them if you remain open to your own life instead of shutting down just because things have changed. Then you start comparing yourself and your life to others.

Putting Holiday Road Band back together in 2003-2004 was possible and exciting. Guitar and vocals from Walter Seaman were and still are one of the highlights of the never-ending Holiday Road Band epic chronicle. Walter and I have been through a few bass players and three drummers. We have a stellar, consistent configuration of Holiday Road Band and we are still rolling on. We play in Iowa now and are quite happy with our fans and the venues. The things that transpired during all those years on the road are much more numerous, and there are so many more tales that I could have written here. Times were fun and not so much fun. They were sparkling and darkly tragic, enlightening, and ridiculous, but all of it was extraordinarily brilliant, and I would do it all again. There is nothing in my life that I ever regretted or wished for. I did the work.

IA Rock and Roll Hall of Fame Induction Ceremony 2016

I love being called "legendary" and "queen of road rock." It's a legacy I have earned from birth.

I never married again because it wasn't for me, especially at such a young age when there was so much for me out in the world. Today, after a couple of uncomfortable, stressful, and controlling relationships that went on for way too long, I have found a soulmate again, and we are perfectly happy. There is mutual respect. Knowing that he respects the fact that I am a free spirit and a strong, independent woman. Being the girl in the band is something he loves about me, too. Those are the things that drew him to me. His kindness,

237

seeing how he treats his mother so well, and his intelligence clinched it for me. Besides, he loves music; he knows everything about bands and musicians and has hosted a radio show in years past.

I have always been solidly comfortable on my own terms and in my own skin, and that is how it will always be. I am surrounded by loving, strong, heroic people, including my family and my friends who are also family. I give them the best part of me every single day because that's how I feel every day. All the days before and everything that happened during those days were meant to be there. It was how I discovered that I was always going to be fine no matter what and no matter where I was or where each path led. And I will always be able to help other people however they need.

They aren't kidding when they tell you each decade is much better than the one before. I've loved, I have been loved, I lost love, I have been independent and worked to stay that way even while being controlled by others to some extent. I was pushed to the edge but always found my way out. I have been a beginner, a teacher of many things, lived life, and survived. I've been a wise woman, a woman who needs no one else to thrive. I have been the other woman, the only woman, and the cheated-on woman, the woman who has had songs and poetry written for her. I've been called a bitch and other hateful things. I have been called talented, caring and giving, strong, a light in the world, and beautiful. I am more of a loner than the life of the party. I've been a friend, a lover, a pain in the ass, a survivor of all things, and a presence. I've been and still am a leader, a caregiver, a lover of beautiful things, a spellcaster, a sister, an aunt, and my mother's daughter. I have always commanded and demanded respect no matter what, and I still do. Above all, I have remained human and kind

At this age, I am younger, wiser, stronger, and just as energetic, positive, and confident as I have always been if not more. I have learned to set boundaries, which is the one thing everyone absolutely should be learning to do. I know the difference between a non-genuine and a genuine person by hearing only one word from them or looking at their faces and into their eyes. Love yourself enough to set your boundaries. Your time and energy are precious and only you get to choose how you use both. Teach people how to treat you by deciding what you will and won't accept for yourself.

I have seen what the ravages of unhealthy lifestyles will do. I lived among musicians and groupies and saw "parties" and wild, careless living, and I was not impressed by that lifestyle. However, I was always impressed with the music we played, the talent of the players, how it felt when my voice burst through the microphone, and how it still feels every single time even now.

Security, strength, self-confidence, and prosperity come from one place, and it is usually the last place most people want to look. It comes from within. It comes from your ability to stand on your own two feet and face yourself in the mirror every day. You must be strong enough to stand alone, smart enough to know when you need help, and brave enough to ask for it.

I feel so lucky to have carried on with this life, meeting and making music and more with some famous folks, helping people get some music into their lives and find the joy it gives. It's such a blessing to help people get healthier and to live a better quality of life. If I have inspired just one person to be healthier, to find and live their passion, then that's perfect. If that one person has inspired one more person, that's even better. I've loved my life - the good and the bad because I never wasted any of it. I used everything that ever happened as something to learn from and move forward.

When you allow yourself to evolve, you realize how dysfunctional everything around you might be. And you won't want to keep playing your part in that dysfunction.

If people weren't dreamers, we wouldn't have the technology, art that stirs the imagination, movies, music, tools, computers, exciting restaurants, clothing, skyscrapers, and a million other things they dreamed of and accomplished because they just went for it no matter what, no matter who balked at the dream. They did whatever it took to make their vision of life real. If they had not discovered their hidden passions or ever said those passions and dreams out loud to anyone, or even said it out loud in a mirror to themselves, then they may never have achieved any of it. Can you imagine going to your grave not having accomplished anything you dreamed of or maybe even just one thing you set out to do in this lifetime because you were afraid, worried, or concerned about what other people may think about you?

How in the world do you even begin to make this accomplishment happen? Choose one thing you want most. Start by speaking up. Tell your family you will accomplish this with or without their help and support (although that would be ideal). Start researching how to do what you want to do. Learn what you need to know and learn as you go. No one knows something automatically. Empower yourself with real knowledge. There is so much information on everything out there. Don't hesitate to speak to people who already do what you wish you were doing. Because one of these days, you'll let time pass, and time will undeniably pass whether you decide to do something or not. Don't wait for it to be easier – it won't, and don't wait for anyone else to do it for you, or you'll be waiting forever.

I've reinvented myself many times throughout my life, not so much with a new look…but with life changes and direction. The one thing that never changes is that I have always stayed true to myself and who I am without excuses. It was tough as a child with heavy, thick glasses and clumsiness. I got teased and made fun of, but I played along. It was part of knowing that I was destined for better things. It got easier as I got through grade school and into high school as my best friends and I shared music and friendship in our "wonder years."

My intentions and attitude have likely been misconstrued from time to time. The main thing that I have learned in all these decades is that the people who choose to live with toxic minds and unhappy lives are the ones who wish their own lives were different but won't take that difficult first step to make change happen. They would rather see the gray instead of the sun. Don't change your life for them or feel as if you need to do something different to please them. You don't. And anything you do to keep trying to please someone else takes time away from who you are and what you want to accomplish.

The best, most valuable thing you can give someone is your time. Nothing is more valuable than time and it cannot be replaced. You can never be replaced.

I wouldn't have missed anything or changed anything for the world.

Dear Shannon,

I thought I would write you a little letter to tell you how much you mean to me. Call me silly but I think there is nothing silly about the care and love I have for you. You do so many thing for me and I really, really apreciate all of them. I hope that I mean alot to you too, cause if I do then that works out so nice for both of us.

Love you Darlin,
Bruce Edward

Shannon 1977   **Perry 1977**

HRB 1985 Jeff R., Shannon, Cindy, Bruce, Roger

HRB 2015 reunion, Roger, Cindy Shannon, Walter

Reader Quotes

"Well, I decided to read "a little bit more" tonight and couldn't stop until I reached the end. What a well-written, wonderful, fascinating, inspirational, instructive and at times heartbreaking story. Really cool historical and first-hand experiences of great music in the 70s and beyond, great stars including your encounters with them and playing and sometimes gigging with them. Also great info about advances in musical instruments, recording equipment, computer technology uses in recordings and formats too. And of course, you have so many compelling stories and impressions of all those people you got to know, some almost seeming angelic, others more like satanic, and some with beautiful later life and some tragic. And you have a consistent theme of always moving ahead. Taking on caregiver responsibilities for a severely ill Bruce, with all the work and stress that such care can involve, taking on additional work to help support that work. And your commitment to life-long learning and advancement in music and so many other passions (martial arts, yoga, fitness training, your other work on helping people improve mental attitude cosmological/astrological studies,....). It's in the end it's also a story of triumph (e.g. IA Rock and Roll Hall Of Fame 2016) and redemption, and your beautiful relationship with Mike G.!"

~Walter Seaman, Emeritus Associate Professor, University of Iowa

"...after reading your story, I can see that you are an amazing, strong woman who has lived and continues to live a life driven by what you believe in. Your life has been filled with so many experiences, good and bad, and your book shows how you used all those experiences to make you the kind, caring, and beautiful person that you are. Your story will definitely help others learn more about how to be true to themselves and become stronger. I only wish I had learned all that you shared when I was younger. I need to remember to use the bad times to help me grow wiser. Yes, I still can use your wisdom to live my life and be the strongest I can be. "

~Yukiko Hill, Educator

"A memoir that truly runs the gamut of a life well and fully lived with feeling and emotions but the number one thing gathered by it all is that you've always lived the life YOU wanted and look back through it with zero regrets. Through the joys, the sorrows, the dangers, and the triumphs, and everything in between. Through it all, your voice is loud and clear, encouraging the reader to make every effort to do the same and making them feel like they CAN do exactly that. I was left with the strong feeling that these are just highlights and that there are more such stories where these came from. I can't wait for you to share more of them."

~Michael Gerstbrein, International DNA Technologies

"Shannon has done an amazing thing here. She has poured out her life onto these pages and taken us along for the ride. She writes well and with passion. Whenever she makes up her mind to do something it gets done, and she has done it all so efficiently!

~Bonnie Hall, Retired Language Educator and lifelong book addict